American Stenciled Quilts

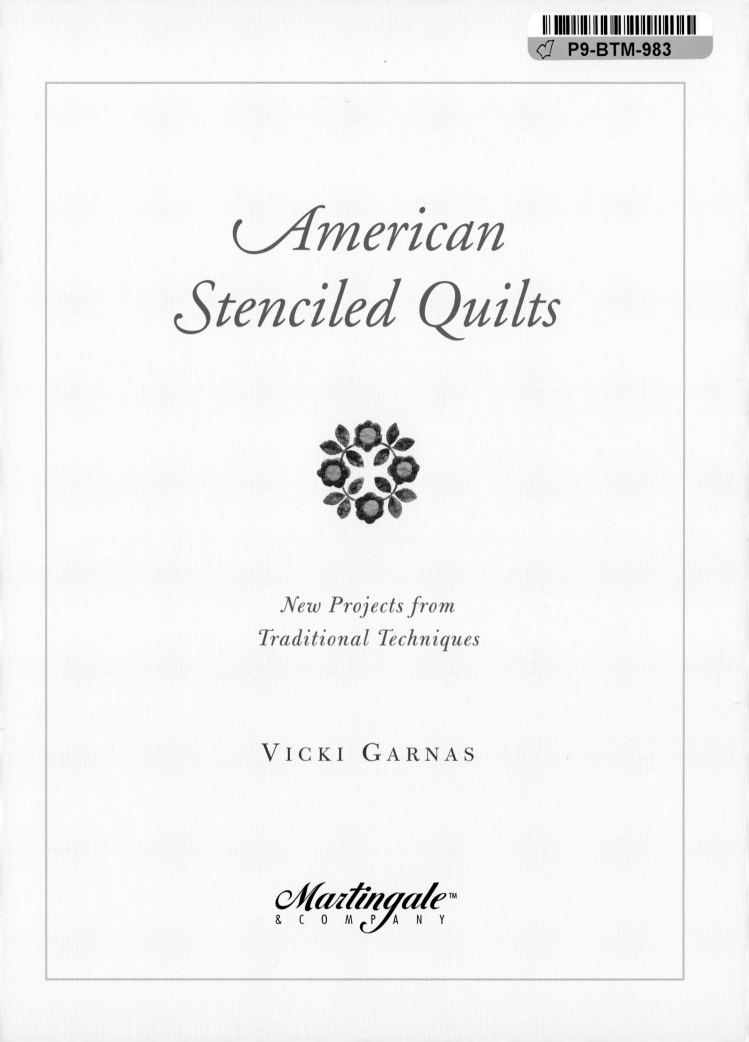

New Projects from
Traditional Techniques

VICKI GARNAS

Martingale™
& COMPANY

Credits

President − − Nancy J. Martin
CEO − − Daniel J. Martin
Publisher − − Jane Hamada
Editorial Director − − Mary V. Green
Managing Editor − − Tina Cook
Technical Editor − − Dawn Anderson
Copy Editor − − Liz McGehee
Design Director − − Stan Green
Illustrator − − Laurel Strand
Cover Designer − − Stan Green
Text Designer − − Regina Girard
Photographer − − Brent Kane

Library of Congress Cataloging-in-Publication Data
Garnas, Vicki
   American stenciled quilts: new projects from
traditional techniques / Vicki Garnas.
      p. cm.
   ISBN 1-56477-461-9
   1. Quilting—Patterns. 2. Stencil work. I. Title.
   TT835 .G3678 2002
   746.46—dc21

                              2002011797

That Patchwork Place® is an imprint
of Martingale & Company™.

American Stenciled Quilts:
   New Projects from Traditional Techniques
© 2002 by Vicki Garnas

Martingale & Company
20205 144th Avenue NE
Woodinville, WA 98072-8478 USA
www.martingale-pub.com

Printed in China
07 06 05 04 03 02   8 7 6 5 4 3 2 1

Mission Statement

We are dedicated to providing quality products
and service by working together to inspire
creativity and to enrich the lives we touch.

Dedication

To my family: Gil, Benjamin, and Matthew. You are God's greatest blessing to me. God bless you.

Acknowledgments

Thank you to the Metropolitan Museum of Art, the Museum of American Folk Art, the Shelburne Museum, the Old Sturbridge Village, and the Winterthur Museum for allowing me to include their quilts in my book—and to all the museums and historical societies who keep our quilt heritage for future generations of quilters.

Special thanks to Mary Green, Tina Cook, and Terry Martin for their help and advice on the book. And thank you to Dawn Anderson for editing the text. You all make me look good!

Contents

Introduction

The early makers of stenciled quilts must have felt the same thrill my students and I feel when stenciling on fabric. It is easy, and the finished appearance is similar to that of an appliquéd quilt. I am not trying to replace the beautiful appliqué method, but I am offering you an alternative approach for achieving a similar look in a lot less time. I prefer the stenciling method over appliqué; I can make lots of quilts quickly and enjoy them sooner.

Many antique stenciled quilts have stenciled designs similar to designs appliquéd on quilts of the same era, showing an innovative crossover of patterns. A woman not skilled in the art of appliqué could create an intricate design of flowers, birds, and leaves, which appeared to be hand sewn when quilted. By using stencils and paint, she could have a quilt top finished in less than half the time of the intricately sewn appliquéd piece. The innovative quilter added hours to her day by stenciling a design instead of sewing it.

Because so few antique stenciled quilts are still in existence, I have also found inspiration for some of my stenciled quilts in appliquéd quilts of the same time period. I love the look of the old appliqué quilts. They have charm, personality, and a quirkiness that gives them great character. The flower placement is not absolutely perfect in every spray of flowers, the colors may differ from block to block, and borders are not the same on all four sides. These are the unexpected characteristics I wanted to give to my quilts. When I began making quilts to represent old quilts, I didn't want to duplicate the quilts exactly, but instead wanted to capture the personality and spirit of the original quilts. Most of my stenciled quilts are smaller than the original antique quilts. I am easily bored and want to get my quilt finished so I can enjoy it. I find it easier to complete lots of different designs when I make smaller quilts, plus I can pack them for travel, teaching, and lectures.

Only one of my quilt patterns is a reproduction of an antique stenciled quilt. The "Nine Patch and Roses" quilt (page 41) represents a quilt stenciled in 1834 by Mary Ann Hoyt. The rest of my designs are based on quilts I have enjoyed in books.

I feel a kinship to the early stencilers in doing something a little on the edge: painting on fabric and turning it into a quilt. Try a stenciled quilt yourself. Learn to cut stencils from freezer paper, stencil the designs onto fabric, and then incorporate them into a quilt. Finally, age the quilt with tea or coffee to duplicate the antique look. I hope you will enjoy this traditional technique for expressing yourself with paint and stencils. The results will be rewarding.

American Stenciled Quilts

Stenciled quilts are rare and humble pieces of our folk-art heritage. Fewer than thirty of these priceless stenciled quilts remain for us to study. It is not known how the stenciled quilts were created, who made them, or why the art died out. One of the primary reasons may have been the dilemma of the paint. Oil paint was expensive, watercolors and dyes washed out, and the typical household paint, although almost indestructible on walls, was destructive to the fabric of the quilt. The availability of good quilting fabric after 1840 was another contributing factor to the death of the stenciled quilt. Times change and so do styles, even in quiltmaking. The mystery of the stenciled quilts, these priceless pieces of American folk art, may never be completely explained. But these unique quilts clearly deserve a place in the history of traditional American quiltmaking.

Early Stenciling in New England

Most stenciled quilts were made between 1820 and 1850 in the New England area of the United States. It does not seem unusual that the quiltmakers of the day incorporated stenciling into their quilting, since it was a popular method of decorating the home and its contents. In the first half of the nineteenth century, men traveled from farm to village throughout New England, offering to stencil homes and businesses for room and board. These itinerant painters carried paint pigments, brushes, and stencils in their saddlebags.

For a few meals and a bed, the painter would fill plain walls with bright, colorful designs that mimicked expensive imported wallpapers. Many of these stenciled walls can still be found in the old houses of New England. These self-taught painters used simply designed stencils cut from oiled paper, leather, or thin tin. They used paint pigments mixed with skimmed milk or linseed oil to make their paints, and applied the bright colors to solid-colored walls with flat, stiff-bristled brushes in simple designs without shading.

Women and Stenciling

The rural woman in the early 1800s fashioned almost everything her family ate, wore, and slept under. Making quilts allowed her to create something beautiful, show off her talent, express her creativity, and keep her family warm. She looked for beauty in the world around her and incorporated it into her everyday life. Humble flower designs were painted onto furniture, tools, and everyday objects.

These homemakers had no art or design training, yet they created beautiful quilts, clothing, and household items. Since many of the early stenciled bedcoverings were not quilted, they could be finished quickly. A spread or counterpane was used to cover a worn quilt or blanket on the bed. Old, homespun bedcoverings could be recycled and made new with some stencils, paints, a brush, and a little ingenuity. The stenciler could stencil the design, finish the edges with fringe or a hem, and have a new bedcovering.

The painted bedcover or quilt was useful and utilitarian in the home. No special care was taken to preserve stenciled quilts; they were used and laundered often. The important, treasured quilts were saved for special times, carefully packed away from daily use. As quilters, we know the tender care and preservation it takes to make textiles last for over 150 years. With time and use, the stenciled quilt wore out and was discarded. Most stenciled quilts were not considered valuable, so little is known about how they were made and by whom. We have only two names attached to antique stenciled quilts: Mary Ann Hoyt, 1834, and Clarissa Moore, 1837. Their names and dates are known because these women stenciled them on their quilts. Unfortunately, little else is known about these imaginative women other than their New England heritage.

Problems with Paint

It is believed that many of the stenciled quilts have not survived because the stenciler probably used paints available on the farm or in the household, left over from painting the house. The caustic paints of the farm would have eaten away the fabric and destroyed the quilts. The colorful paints lasted hundreds of years on the walls and furniture, but devastated the quilts stenciled with them. If the quilter tried to use vegetable dyes or less-caustic paints to create her quilt, it would not stand up to washing unless she combined the dyes with a mordant to make them more durable. To produce a thick, durable paint, colorful pigments had to be mixed with a liquid, such as oil or skimmed milk.

Developments in Early Stenciling

Young ladies were often taught to stencil theorem pictures in female seminaries. These pictures used a stenciled formula for the arrangements of fruit or flowers on velvet and were painted with oil paint or watercolors. Using stencils and simple techniques for applying paint, young women were ensured they could create lovely, still-life pictures with little artistic ability.

Birds and butterflies were often added, and details were applied with a brush. Some of the designs on priceless antique stenciled quilts resemble the overflowing baskets found in these stenciled theorem pictures (see "Theorem Stenciled Baskets" on page 56).

The earliest stenciled quilts resemble the embroidered quilts and the appliquéd *broderie perse* quilts, popular years earlier in the American Colonies. The early whole-cloth embroidered quilts had a large design surrounded by smaller motifs and an embroidered border. "Pot of Flowers Spread," c.1825–35, on page 10, is an example of a whole-cloth stenciled quilt that resembles the earlier embroidered quilts. Whole-cloth stenciled quilts were rarely quilted. Most of the whole-cloth quilts I have seen have fringe or hem tape on a single layer of fabric. These early stenciled quilts show the use of single-motif stencils. By grouping and regrouping single-flower and leaf stencils, a stenciler could form a complete floral spray or lengthen a branch to hold a bird or more flowers and leaves.

Unfinished Pot of Flowers, 2001, Vicki Garnas, 22" x 22". Arrangement of flowers in a basket or urn was a common design for stenciled walls, furniture, and quilts. The rippled flowers are found on several stenciled quilts; their variations were used in early appliqué quilts.

The single-motif-stencil method is easy to spot since it was difficult to create a perfectly symmetrical design. Mistakes and small areas were touched up and covered with brushwork after the stenciling was complete. These early stenciled quilts are true folk art, made by untrained, unknown artists who relied on their own instinct to create an overall balanced design on the finished quilt.

As stenciled quilts progressed, the stencils became more intricate. By the 1830s, precut stencils were available, and the stenciled designs had a uniform look. The stenciler no longer had to build a bouquet of flowers from individual flowers, leaves, and stems. Instead, she could use a complete bouquet stencil. Designs began to look like the theorem stencils of abundant overflowing flowers and fruit. "Stenciled Quilt of Plain and Printed Cottons," c. 1820–50, on page 12, shows several distinct

stenciled designs surrounded by an 1830s red-and-brown, roller-printed cotton. This quilt may have been a sampler of the stenciler's designs, created to display her variety of stencils and innovative talent.

Eventually, the stenciler used her paint and stencils to make designs that were combined with patchwork blocks. "Nine-Patch Stenciled Quilt" by Mary Ann Hoyt, 1834, on page 13, is a pieced and stenciled quilt. Mary Ann used the simple Nine Patch quilt block and a stenciled rose design to make the body of her quilt. Three outside edges of the quilt have a basket with flowers stenciled in the plain squares. The baskets of roses and leaves appear to have been built up one motif at a time. The roses in the rest of the quilts' squares have a uniformity, suggesting a complete stencil rather than a buildup of motifs.

Common Designs

The inventive stenciler found designs in many sources, just as the quilter looked to different areas for her patterns. Generalized patterns were rare in quilting during the early part of the nineteenth century. Patterns for quilting, appliqué, and stitchery were passed from hand to hand. Women traded patterns by drawing them off other quilts, fabrics, or wallpapers. Flowers, leaves, pots, birds, stars, and animals were common motifs found in quilts of all kinds. Some of the flower patterns used in stencils and quiltmaking came from nature and are simplistic rather than realistic. The rose seems to be the most popular motif in stenciled quilts, although the style of the flower varies greatly. Designs were simplified and made easier to sew or cut out for stenciling. The rose pattern is a perfect example of a simplified design. The early 1800s found the rose as a six- or eight-petal flower with a circle for the center. Stencils of the same designs can be found on walls in New England. Leaves were shaped with uneven edges, or were cut in smooth, simple designs.

*Pot of Flowers Stenciled Spread, quiltmaker unidentified; New England;
1825–1835; cotton, handmade cotton fringe on three sides, and paint. Collection of
the American Folk Art Museum, New York. Gift of George E. Schoellkopf, 1978.12.1.*

This quilt is a whole-cloth spread with fringe on three sides. It is stenciled in red, green, blue, and gold and resembles embroidered spreads and quilts of the era. The style is symmetrical, with sprays of flowers and trees that make up a balanced composition. The center basket of flowers and leaves includes a bird and was built up using several separate stencils. The starlike motif is actually a flower surrounded by leaves. This same type of motif, built up into a complete pattern, is seen on *broderie perse* quilts in the early-nineteenth century. Many of the flower designs can be found in fabric, wallpaper, and other quilts of the same era.

Block-Work Stenciled Spread; possibly Sara Massey; possibly Watertown,
New York; 1825–1840, cotton and paint, 76¼" x 88". Collection of the
American Folk Art Museum, New York. Gift of Robert Bishop, 1985.37.9.

This quilt, unlike the floral whole-cloth quilts, resembles a twelve-block quilt with sashing and borders. The squares are stenciled in an Oak Leaf and Reel pattern with flower details. Its red and green coloring and simple stenciling make a charming top. There appear to be at least four different stencils used in the twelve squares; changing the color placement provides variety. The reel stencil squares seem to be made from a whole stencil, while the floral sprays in the top row are more free-form and were probably built up separately. The border is a repetition of small leaves with a flower center. The sashing is stenciled to resemble fabric. The floral motifs are similar to the flowers found in both of the floral whole-cloth quilts from the same period. Although made to resemble an appliquéd quilt, put together with fabric sashing, this quilt is beautiful in its nonconformity.

Stenciled Quilt of Plain and Printed Cottons, unknown maker, c. 1820–50, 62" x 78",
probably New Hampshire, Old Sturbridge Village collection, 26.23.175. Photo by Henry E. Peach.

This quilt is pieced with stenciled cotton and linen squares and roller-printed 1830s red and brown squares. It appears to be a sampler of the stenciler's multitude of stencils. The stencil technique and shading suggest a theorem-trained stenciler. She corrected and touched up her stencils with paint and a brush. This talented woman stenciled many different flowers, birds, leaves, butterflies, and even a cat in her solid-colored squares. The quilt squares are set on point, quilted simply, and bound with a plain binding. This handsome quilt tells of a clever and resourceful maker.

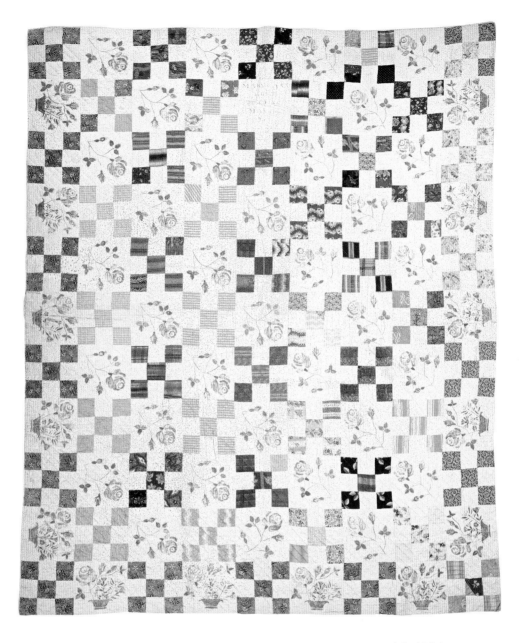

Nine-Patch Stenciled Quilt, Mary Ann Hoyt, May 15, 1834,
73" x 86½", Reading, Pennsylvania. Courtesy, Winterthur Museum.

This quilt is clearly identified because Mary Ann stenciled her name, place, and the date on the quilt. Stenciling was a common way to add a name to a quilt in the 1800s. Signature and album quilts made in the same era often had names stenciled on them. The Nine Patch quilt also has the number 2 stenciled in the identification block on the front of the quilt. It seems to indicate that Mary Ann stenciled at least one other quilt like this. The uniformity of the stenciled red rose, leaves, and buds in the plain cotton squares suggests a commercially cut stencil. The "border" of red roses, flowers, and green leaves massed in the blue and gold basket seem to be made up of single-motif stencils; they are not uniform in the arrangement of flowers. Mary Ann combined her stenciled roses with roller-printed cottons pieced into Nine Patch blocks in a straight set. There is a peculiar arrangement of the rose design in the quilt: the basket blocks all face into the quilt, but the arrangement of the stenciled rose design varies throughout the quilt. The quilting was done in diagonal lines. The quilter's stenciled flowers and identification makes this humble design a rare piece of folk art.

Fabric for Stenciled Quilts

Antique stenciled quilts were made from plain and printed fabrics. I made my quilts using simple muslin and printed cottons to replicate the tones and appearance of the materials used in earlier times. Use the colors and fabrics you love, from plain plaids to large prints, to create a stenciled quilt just for you.

Muslin

Muslin is plain woven cotton for domestic use. It has been used for backgrounds and quilt backings for decades. Quilters who appliqué a lot advise against using unbleached musin for backgrounds. However, I love muslin and I recommend using it for the background of my stenciled quilts. I like the unrefined look of the uneven weave and the brown specks. I also like muslin because it wrinkles and shrinks making the stencils pop out. Let me make a stand for unassuming, unbleached, and plain-weave fabrics. They make super stenciled quilts!

I did a little research to see just what types of muslin are available to the quilter today. One of the main problems with muslin is its variance in quality. I checked twenty-three different types of muslin or muslinlike fabrics, searching it out in a major chain of fabric stores, in quilt shops, through mail-order sources, and on the Internet. The prices I found for muslin ranged from ninety-nine cents a yard to almost eight dollars a yard. The range of quality is almost as vast, from a loose-weave cheesecloth variety to ones with very closely woven threads. After conducting my own research and talking to quilters, shop owners, and manufacturers, my advice is: use what you like best!

Many quilt stores have a muslin called *dyer's muslin*. This type of muslin is not treated with a surface finish, so it will accept the dye when exposed to the dye vat. Although dyer's muslin is found in a lot of quilt stores, you don't need to go to the extra expense of purchasing it for your stenciled quilt. It is not necessary to buy the most expensive muslin, but please don't buy the least expensive variety either. At a large-chain fabric store, I found many types of fabric under the muslin category. I tested a ninety-nine-cents-a-yard muslin by washing and drying it in the dryer. This muslin shrinks considerably and wrinkles up too much to iron flat for use in a stenciled quilt. It was only 36" wide to begin with and shrunk at least 2" in width and length when washed. Please don't use this type for your stenciled quilt. Instead, look for one with a tight weave that is still rather homespun in appearance, with the brown specks in it.

At my local store, I purchase muslin made specifically for quilters in the middle of the muslin price range. This muslin is 44" to 45" wide, 100% cotton, and natural in color. When washed, the fabric does shrink a little and has a wrinkled appearance that is easy to smooth when ironed. This muslin is the one I like to use, and quilting through it is very easy.

Another one of my favorite muslins to stencil on is 100% cotton, 44" to 45" wide with a thread count of 78 x 78. Thread count is the number of threads found in 1" of fabric going both ways. Thread count of 78 x 78 means there are 78 threads going one direction and 78 threads crossing in the other direction in each inch of fabric. If you put the fabric under a magnifying glass, you could actually count the threads. Most quilting cottons have a thread count of 90 or higher. Sheeting and broadcloth have around 200 threads per inch. The higher the thread count in muslin, the stiffer and heavier the texture and feel of the fabric. Since I like to hand quilt my stenciled quilts, I don't like the 200-count muslin because it is too difficult to hand quilt through.

Don't forget to look at the solid-colored quilting fabrics. Some stores have a natural or "classic" type of cloth that resembles muslin without the brown specks, but with the same texture and feel. When I washed this fabric, it had a little shrinkage and wrinkling, but ironed smooth. I like this type of cloth to give a more refined and finished look to the quilts.

So, armed with this information, go to your favorite quilt store, fabric store, Internet site, or mail-order catalog and ask about muslin. Tell them you want a good-quality muslin for an antique-looking quilt. Take a close look at the types and varieties of muslin available in your store. Look closely at the weave. Can you see spaces in between the threads more in one fabric than the other? Take the fabric in your hand and feel it. Does it feel coarse and stiff, or smooth and soft? Muslin has a slightly rough texture, yet it feels soft when crinkled in your hand. Choose the fabric you like the best, take it home, and wash it. (I wash my muslin before stenciling, but not the rest of my fabric.) Then get ready to stencil that plain cotton into something extraordinary.

Printed Background for Stenciling

The stenciled quilts I have seen from the 1800s were stenciled on plain fabric. I like to stencil on printed fabric for variety. Printed muslins and cottons are wonderful for stenciling. The little designs show up through the paint and give a secondary texture to the stenciled design. It just adds a little more interest to the quilt.

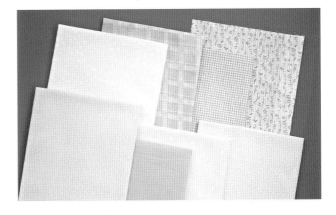

Some of the different background choices are plain, printed, tone-on-tone, and plaid.

As long as the print doesn't dominate the stenciled design, I like it. Turn some of your fabrics over and check the back, too. It is fun to stencil on the fronts and backs of the same fabric to add more variety in your quilt. By using both sides of the fabric, you can double the number of fabrics you have.

You can use both the fronts and backs of fabrics for variation and more textural choices.

Recipe for Print Fabrics in Stenciled Quilts

I use print fabrics for accents in many of my stenciled quilts. Some of the antique stenciled quilts incorporated different kinds of fabrics or combined pieced blocks with stenciled squares. I have chosen a scrap look for the fabric pieces I have added to my stenciled designs. Don't feel you have to choose fabrics that accurately reflect a specific time period. Throw in a lot of fabrics to add color and variety to your quilt.

Picking a Fabric Palette

Antique stenciling relied on basic paint colors and pigments of the time. Red, green, yellow ochre, brown, black, and a few blues were the main colors found in stenciled designs. Since pigments were mixed for the painting, the simple colors were dominant. I have chosen to stay true to these colors in most of my fabric choices. This makes it easy to choose fabrics to go with the stenciled pieces. Red, blue, green, gold, brown, and black are the main fabric colors I paired with my stenciled designs. But that doesn't mean just the basic colors. It includes a wide range of tones from light to dark and dull to bright, plus a wide range of fabric patterns.

Quilters in the 1800s used what was on hand to make their quilts, so not everything matched in color or tone. Stir some brighter tones into the mix, such as bluish green, bright red, or gold. These colors need to be used more than once in the quilt to keep the eye moving throughout the design. Since the quilts I make are not exact copies of the quilts of a certain period, I like to use a variety of fabrics. This way, I can use both what I have and what tempts me at the quilt shop.

Stenciling in the Twenty-First Century

The paints we use now are perfect for stenciling quilts. The women who stenciled antique quilts would have used paints intended for exterior use on houses, barns, or farm tools. These paints, made from organic pigments, contained large amounts of salt, iron, and lead. The paints were corrosive and ate the fabric they were stenciled on, destroying the quilts. The choices available at that time included oil paint, watercolors, fabric dyes, or household paints.

With the materials now available in the twenty-first century, including fabrics, freezer paper, paint sponges, and pens, you can make a stenciled quilt to rival the antique stenciled quilt of the nineteenth century. Using any of the stencil patterns in the book makes it easy.

Freezer Paper

A stencil is a template made by cutting a window or hole in a stencil material. Stencilers in the nineteenth century cut their stencils from a variety of stencil materials, including oiled paper, leather, tin, and wax-covered linen. If the stencil material was too thick, the paint could seep under the stencil, causing a sloppy edge. Today, I prefer to make all my stencils from freezer paper. Freezer paper is perfect for stenciling on fabric, since it can be ironed onto the fabric and stabilizes it. Stencil cutting is the hardest part of the whole process, so if you can cut the paper, the rest is a breeze.

Paints

Can you imagine making your own paints by grinding color pigment and mixing it with oil? That is what early stencilers had to do. Each color pigment was crushed to a fine powder, and then oil, milk, or another liquid was slowly added and mixed with the pigment until the proper consistency was achieved.

Today we have hundreds of colors of paint already mixed and ready to stencil with. I love the acrylic craft paints readily available at the craft and fabric stores, and I use the paint straight from the bottle. The acrylic paint cleans up easily with water. Quilts stenciled with acrylic paint are washable, and all my quilts are washed. The paint even withstands the harsh treatment I use when I age the quilts with tea or coffee. Fabric dyes are more expensive and I don't find the need for them unless the piece is to be washed regularly. Because dyes are absorbed into the fabric rather than sitting on the surface as paint does, they are less likely to change color or be removed when a quilt is washed often.

You have many acrylic paints to choose from.

Sponges and Brushes

Stencilers in the nineteenth century used brushes called *scrubs* that were much like the stencil brushes we use today. Stencilers also used pieces of fabric wound around their fingers to stencil with oil paints and watercolors on fabric. Sponges are my first choice. Cosmetic sponge wedges found at the discount stores are my favorite; I buy them by the basketful. Sponges are inexpensive and easy to use, and I can throw them away when I am done.

Brushes are expensive and have to be cleaned after use, but buy some to use in the large stencil openings. You should not wash the brushes to use them for more than one color, so have several on hand. I suggest 1" or ¾" brushes for large stencil openings. You can use brushes for the large openings and sponges for the smaller areas on the same stencil.

Use brushes or cosmetic sponges for stenciling.

Stenciling Basics

To stencil, you fill in the opening in a freezer-paper stencil with paint. It is simple and, with the use of freezer paper, almost foolproof. Don't be afraid to give it a try. The biggest mistake new stencilers make is using too much paint. You don't want to completely paint the surface. The goal is to color it but allow a little of the background fabric to show through the paint.

Stencil Terms Defined

Every technique has its own language. To make and use stencils effectively, it helps to know what the different parts are called. Below is a sketch of a stencil with the parts labeled.

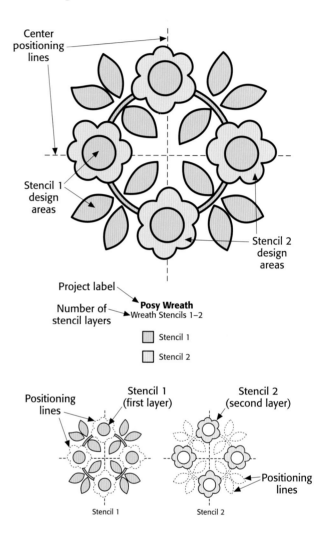

Positioning lines: dashed lines used for positioning a stencil on the background fabric.

Project label: the name of the design or project.

Stencil design area: designates the hole that is cut from the paper. It is the area you remove to make the stencil.

Stencil (noun): freezer paper with the design area cut out, ready to fuse to the background fabric and paint.

Stencil (verb): to dab the paint in the hole or stencil design area.

Stenciler: YOU, after you use this book!

Making the Stencil

You'll need:

> Freezer paper
> Pencil
> Cuticle scissors or craft knife
> Rotary cutter, acrylic ruler, and cutting mat
> Black marker

Directions

Some of the stencil patterns for the quilts in this book are oversized and printed on more than one page. Other stencil patterns have been reduced to fit on a page and will need to be enlarged on a photocopy machine. For these patterns you will need to tape sections together to make a master pattern (refer to "The Master Pattern" on page 20). You will make your stencil pattern from the master pattern, following the directions below. If you are using a pattern printed actual size, you can trace it onto your freezer paper directly from the book.

1. Most of the designs in this book are stenciled in layers. The stencil patterns are color-coded so you can see which design areas to cut for a given stencil. Determine how many stencils you need to cut for your design (in the case of the Posy Wreath sample, two). For each stencil, cut a piece of freezer paper as indicated in the project directions. (I use a dull rotary cutter, mat, and ruler.)

2. Center the freezer paper on top of the pattern or master pattern, dull side up, and trace the entire design with a pencil. Be sure to include the dashed center positioning lines. Repeat for any subsequent stencils; for example, the Posy Wreath calls for two stencils, so you would need to make two tracings. Be sure to include dashed positioning lines on subsequent stencil layers to line up stencils with stenciled designs.

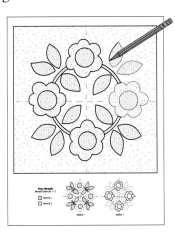

3. Write the pattern name and the stencil number (i.e., stencil 1, stencil 2) on each tracing.

4. To cut out small design areas, I prefer to use cuticle scissors. For larger areas, I use a craft knife and rotary-cutting mat. First poke a hole in the center of the design area. Do not cut from the outside edge of the paper into the traced area. Cut inside the design only, leaving the surrounding area uncut. In this example, you would cut out the pink shapes (leaves, vines, and flower centers) for stencil 1 and the apricot shapes (flowers) for stencil 2.

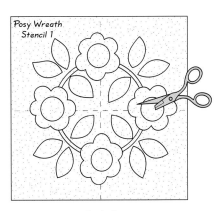

Poke hole.

Cut along traced line.

Freezer-paper stencils can be used up to six times. Simply peel off and re-fuse to the fabric.

The Master Pattern

You'll need:
- Paper
- Ruler
- Pencil
- Transparent tape
- Black marker

Directions

Some of the stencil patterns for the quilts in this book are oversized and printed in sections on more than one page. For those designs, you will need to trace each of the sections and tape them together to make a master pattern in order to trace your stencil from a single pattern. Other stencil patterns have been reduced to fit on the page. For those designs, you will need to enlarge the patterns on a photocopy machine and tape the pieces together to make a master pattern.

1. For patterns printed in sections, make the master pattern by tracing each of the design sections onto paper. For reduced patterns, enlarge the pattern on a photocopy machine as indicated on the pattern.

2. Lay out the design sections, overlapping as necessary to complete the pattern.

3. Tape the pieces together to form a single pattern. For traced patterns, retrace the pencil lines with black pen to make them easier to see.

4. This completes the master pattern. Make the stencil for the master pattern, following "Making the Stencil" on page 19.

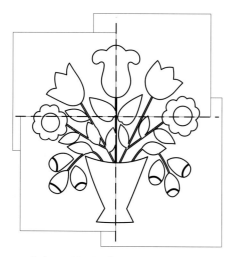

Include positioning lines, any joining lines, and labels on your pattern.

Applying the Paint

You'll need:
- Fabric
- Iron and ironing board
- Freezer-paper stencils
- Acrylic craft paint
- Paper plate
- Paper towels
- Cosmetic sponge wedges

Directions

1. Cut a piece of fabric to the size indicated in the project directions. For blocks, fold the fabric in half and in half again, crease, and unfold. For border pieces, fold the short ends together and crease in the center; then unfold.

2. Set iron on "cotton" with no steam. Place the fabric right side up on the ironing board. Lay stencil 1 shiny side down on the fabric, matching the center positioning lines on the stencil to the creases on the fabric.

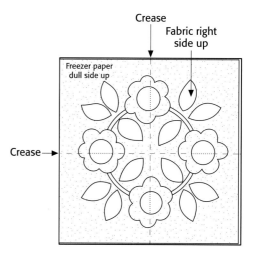

Place positioning lines at creases.

3. Iron the stencil to the fabric. This takes about 30 seconds. Test the edges from time to time and stop when they are fused.

4. Place a piece of freezer paper on your work surface to protect it. Pour a tablespoon of the desired paint color on a paper plate. Fold a piece of paper towel in half and put it next to the paper plate.

5. Grasp a dry sponge on the opposite sides with your thumb and index finger so the large surface is down. The exposed area at the bottom of the sponge will be your painting surface.

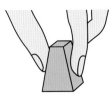

6. Dip the sponge into the paint. Blot on the paper towel to remove excess paint and work the paint onto the sponge until the paint on the towel looks dull. Stenciling is a dry brush technique; too much paint means a sloppy stencil.

7. Hold the fabric down with your free hand to stabilize it. Still holding the sponge on the sides with your other hand, begin applying the paint around the edge of the stencil opening. Use either an up-and-down motion, called *stippling,* or a round-and-round motion, called *rouging.* Add more paint as needed, always remembering to blot the paper towel before applying the sponge to the fabric. Gradually work toward the center of the opening with the same motion until the fabric is covered. Keep the paint at the center of the design a little lighter than that at the outside edges. You don't want to conceal the fabric surface totally; just cover with color and create a crisp edge. To add another color to the design, use another sponge. Continue stenciling in the same manner until all the open areas are filled in with paint.

8. When the design is complete, carefully peel off the stencil.

9. Wait until the first layer is dry (usually in a minute or so); then place stencil 2 on the painted design so that the traced lines match up with the outlines of the areas you've already painted. Place a paper towel over the new stencil and press to fuse. Remove the paper towel.

10. Stencil the second stencil in the same manner. Use a fresh sponge for each color; start with the edges and work toward the center of the openings. Continue stenciling any additional layers in the same manner as for stencil 2. When you pull off the stencil and reveal the painted areas, the finished design will be fresh and crisp.

To stencil with a brush, follow the same method as for a sponge, but hold your brush upright in the paint. Blot on the paper towel to remove excess paint. Begin to rouge the paint onto the stencil with a round-and-round motion at the edge of the cutout, moving on into the center of the stencil. Use a different brush for each color. You can use both brushes and sponges on the same design, using sponges for the smaller cutout areas, and brushes for the larger areas.

Heat-Setting Your Stenciled Design

Cover your ironing board with a press cloth, paper, or muslin to protect it. Place the painted surface facedown on the press cloth. To heat-set the acrylic paint, iron the back of the fabric with a dry iron set on "cotton" for one minute. Ironing on the back first sets the paint the best. Turn the stencil piece over, cover the painted surface with paper or muslin, and iron the front for another minute or two.

Fabric dyes can also be heat-set by drying in the dryer on high or cotton setting for twenty minutes.

Outlining for a Better Design

Antique stenciled quilt designs were not outlined, but most of mine are. "Nine Patch and Roses" (page 41) is the only quilt in this book on which I have not outlined my stenciled design. Some of the antique quilts' stenciled designs were touched up with paint and a brush to complete or fill in areas of the stencils.

I like to complete the open areas of the stencil with pen outline; to me, this brings character and life to the stencil. You don't have to know how to draw or even draw a straight line; just follow the outline of the paint. I recommend the Sharpie pen in both the fine and ultra fine points. I think a Sharpie pen is the best because it is inexpensive and doesn't clog with paint when I scribble over the stenciled surface. I also like the dark black line the Sharpie pen makes. The Sharpie pen says "not for cloth," but I use them all the time. Test for bleeding on a scrap of your quilt fabric first. I don't mind some bleeding and consider it part of the folk-art look of the quilt. Test the pen, and if the ink bleeds too much for your taste, either use a pen designed for fabric writing (generally more expensive) or keep the Sharpie pen on the painted surface.

Other pens to consider are the Zig, Marvy, and Y&C FabricMate with pigment ink or permanent ink. I use black for all my outlining.

Black Permanent Marking Pens
and a Test Sample on Muslin

1. Place a piece of paper under the fabric in case the ink bleeds through the fabric. Test the pen on a scrap of fabric for bleeding.
2. Draw a broken, uneven line around the stenciled area, keeping the pen either on the painted surface or right at the edge. You can feel the edge of the paint with the pen.
3. Use the pen to fill in where the painted areas do not quite connect, such as where a leaf is not connected to the stem.
4. Draw design lines as necessary on the interior of the stenciled areas, such as vein lines on leaves, using the stencil pattern and project photos as guides for line placement.

Pen-Work Detailing on Posy Wreath Block

Sewing and Finishing Your Quilt

These quilts are designed to make the stenciled images stand out. Most of the quilts are simply constructed, with few pieces and straight borders. Quilting is also kept easy, usually limited to outline quilting around the stenciled designs, with a grid of diamonds overall, so most of the quilting is simple for the beginner.

Borders

Mitered borders are a rare find in antique quilts from the New England area during the 1820s–40s. Fabric was used carefully to avoid waste, and quilters used seamed borders, not mitered ones. I like the simple look and do not like to miter corners.

I've calculated the border length for some quilts based on what it should be when ¼" seams are used throughout. As you know, not everyone sews a perfect ¼" seam, including me. So please measure your own quilt blocks and quilt top across the center after they are sewn together to make sure your borders are cut the right size. Measuring your piece will ensure borders that fit and a quilt that lies flat.

Follow the steps below to add borders.

1. Begin by measuring across the center of the piece from top to bottom. Cut 2 border strips this length, piecing as necessary.

2. Pin the border strips to the sides of the quilt top, matching centers and ends; stitch. Press seam allowances toward the border.

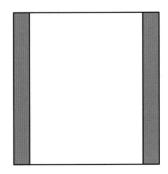

Side Borders

3. Measure across the center of the quilt top from side to side, including the side border strips just added. Cut 2 border strips to this length, piecing as necessary.

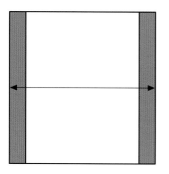

4. Pin the border strips to the top and bottom edges of the quilt, matching centers and ends; stitch. Press the seam allowances toward the border.

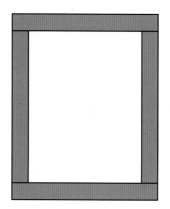

Top and Bottom Borders

Batting

I like the quilt to look flat but still have some loft when I quilt around the stenciled design. I have found cotton batting consistently gives this result. I don't prewash the batting. I just take it out of the bag, unfold it, and let it relax before I baste the quilt.

Basting

This is my least favorite part of the quilting process, and I usually use safety pins to baste my quilts.

I begin in the center and pin my way around the quilt's motifs and seams to hold the three layers together. I space my pins 4" to 5" apart.

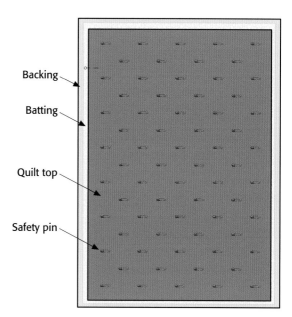

I fold the backing around to the front of the quilt and baste it down over the exposed batting to protect the raw edges as I quilt in the hoop. I drag my quilts everywhere to hand quilt them and have had no problem with the pins keeping the layers safe and secure.

Quilt Marking

I mark the designs on my quilt with a No. 2 pencil. This is the way most early-American quiltmakers would have marked their quilts. I find that after the design is quilted and tea-dyed, the pencil marks are obscured.

Most of my stenciled quilts use straight-line quilting through the background. This is the way the simple antique stenciled quilts were quilted. Masking tape is an easy way to make straight lines. To find masking tape in different sizes, try hardware or paint stores; they have a variety of sizes. I like the blue painter's tape because it doesn't harm the painted design when I pull it off the quilt.

Quilting

I love to hand quilt my stenciled designs. Hand quilting is relaxing and peaceful to me, like prayer time. I like to outline quilt around the stenciled motifs to make them pop up, enhancing the designs. After quilting around the stenciled motifs, I also add quilting lines to the backgrounds of my quilts. My preferred background quilting design is an overall quilted diamond pattern.

Follow the steps below to quilt a diamond pattern.

1. Position a piece of masking tape diagonally across the center of the quilt, aligning one edge with the corners and center of the quilt. Quilt along both sides of the masking tape, skipping over the stenciled design. I like to quilt from the center outward.

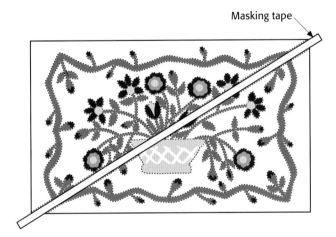

Masking tape

2. Remove the tape and reposition along one of the quilted lines. Quilt along the remaining long edge of the tape to make parallel quilted lines. Repeat over the entire quilt.
3. Tape across the quilt on the diagonal in the opposite direction and repeat the quilting process to make a quilted diamond pattern.

Binding Your Quilt

Early-American quilts were usually bound with a woven tape or plain binding. I have found that straight-grain binding looks like the bindings of early quilts. This binding method is simple and keeps the quilt flat and square. Cutting bindings on the straight of the grain saves fabric and time, both of which nineteenth-century quilters would have appreciated.

I have entered several of my stenciled quilts in shows, and the judges have often commented on the neatness, the finished corners, and how well the binding fits the quilt. Try this method and see if it doesn't result in prizewinning bindings.

1. After the quilting is finished, press the edges of your quilt top. Using a rotary cutter and ruler, trim the batting and backing even with the quilt-top edges. Use your ruler to make sure the corners are square. Trim as necessary.
2. Cut binding strips 2" wide.
3. Measure through the center of your quilt top from top to bottom. Cut 2 binding strips to this length.

4. With right sides together and binding strips on top, pin the binding to the sides of the quilt top. Make sure the short ends of the binding are even with the edges of the quilt. Gently stretch binding as necessary to fit the quilt top.

Pin.

5. Stitch a ¼" seam from top to bottom on both sides. Press the seam allowances toward the binding.

Stitch.

6. Turn the quilt over and fold the long raw edges of the bindings to meet the raw edges of the quilt.

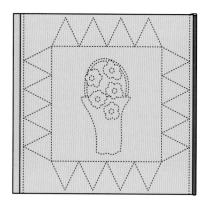

7. Fold in the bindings again, bringing the folded edges over the seam allowances to cover the stitching on the quilt back. Press. Pin at both ends while holding the folded edges flat against the quilt back.

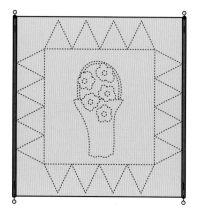

8. Measure across the center of the quilt from side to side, including the binding strips just added. Add 3½" to this measurement and cut 2 binding strips this length.

9. Fold the quilt in half lengthwise to determine the centers of the top and bottom edges; pin-mark. Fold the 2 binding strips from step 8 in half crosswise to determine their centers; crease to mark.

10. Pin the binding to the top and bottom edges of the quilt top, right sides together, matching center creases and pin marks. Fold the ends of the top and bottom bindings to the back of the quilt, over the pinned side bindings. Pin in place, making sure the ends are wrapped tightly around the edges of the quilt.

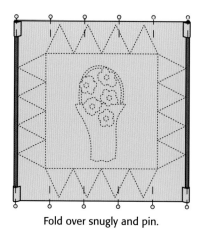

Fold over snugly and pin.

11. Sew from one folded-over edge to the other, backstitching at the ends and sewing through all layers. Use a ¼" seam allowance. Remove all pins.

12. Fold the top and bottom binding strips away from the quilt, turning the wrapped ends right side out. Press.

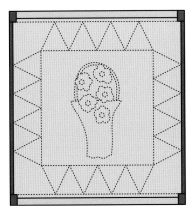

Turn bindings right side out and press.

13. Fold, press, and pin the top and bottom bindings as described in steps 6 and 7 on page 26.

14. Hand stitch the binding down, making sure it covers the stitching lines on the back.

Hand stitch binding on wrong side.

Labeling Your Quilt

The makers of antique stenciled quilts are only known because they stenciled their names on their quilts. Stencil your name on your quilt or make a stenciled label with your name, the date, plus your city and state. I like to take a motif from the quilt and stencil it on muslin. Then I add the information with a Sharpie pen. Label your quilts so others will know who made them and when.

Aging Your Quilt

I have experimented with a lot of different techniques to age my quilts, from fading fabric to using fabric dyes. I like the puckery, aged look that tea dyeing gives my new stenciled quilts.

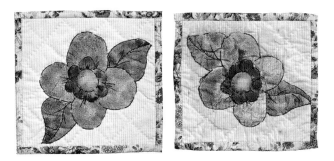

Un-aged piece and aged piece. I like the spots and uneven tone tea and coffee give my quilts.

To me, the staining completes my American stenciled quilt. Tea and coffee have traditionally been used by women to give instant age to fabrics. I like the unevenness and ease of tea dyeing in making my new quilts look old. Tea and coffee are semipermanent, meaning I can re-wash a quilt to lighten it if it turns too dark in the tea bath.

Most aging directions recommend dyeing large chunks of fabric with tea or tan dye before you make the quilt. Since I want the whole quilt aged, paint and all, I wait until the quilting and binding are done. This way, the tea covers everything and I can spot or stain the quilted surface as I like. The painted areas take on an uneven tone with tea dyeing, instantly aging them. Since I use unbleached muslin for the background of my stenciled quilts, the tea staining adds another textured layer to the design.

My approach to quiltmaking is to have fun and make something I can finish and enjoy. Because my goals are temporal, I do things for the immediate gratification with no thought to how long it will last. Yes, tea will eventually wash out, and the tannic acid might hurt the fabric in the long run, but I am not concerned with it. I like the look, and this is the easiest way I have found to age my designs. I like surprises; I'm never sure how the quilt will turn out. Try it yourself on a small project and see if you like it. I have no true recipe for dyeing, but usually I use tea, with instant coffee for the age spots. Tea bags are the easiest to use and the cheapest ones are the best because they usually give the fabric a brown tone. Some teas produce more of a pink or orange tone. I use a large enamel bowl for the dyeing, but any vessel will work. I don't like working with hot water, so I dilute the tea with warm water. That way I can make this a hands-on method.

Follow the steps below to try tea dyeing.

1. Fill a quart jar with water and 7 tea bags. Heat in the microwave for 5 minutes. Let the tea steep for 15 minutes or until water is warm (not hot).

2. Pour tea mixture and bags into a large pan of water and stir. Add another quart of warm water.

3. Add your quilt to the tea mixture. I usually ball up the quilt and stuff it into the pan of tea. Move it around, mushing the liquid, tea bags, and quilt together with your hands. Let it stand for about 10 minutes.

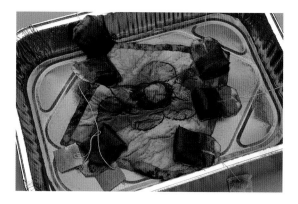

Squish up the quilt in the tea mixture to age.

4. Remove the quilt from the tea bath and rinse under running water, squeezing out the excess. Your quilt will have an aged look. If it is not dark enough, put it through the tea bath once more.

5. Lay the quilt on an old towel and roll to remove the excess water, or wring it out. Wringing out your quilt gives it a wrinkled, aged appearance. Wrapping it in a towel makes the quilt smoother and less distressed. At this point, decide if you want to stay with the look you have or to age it even more.

6. To give the quilt a further appearance of age, lay the quilt on a towel on a flat surface and add spots with a tea bag, instant-coffee granules, or both. Squeeze tea bags on the quilt and rub an area of the quilt with a wet tea bag, pressing it into the fabric. Sprinkle instant-coffee granules on the quilt's wet surface for age spots, mashing the granules into the fabric. Let the quilt sit for a while with the tea and/or coffee on the top.

To add more age to the quilt, place a wet tea bag on the wet quilt and dot with instant-coffee granules.

7. Remove the tea bags and shake off the coffee and tea leaves left on the quilt top. Either put the quilt in the dryer with a couple of old towels for 15 minutes to dry or hang up to dry naturally. Your quilt will come out wrinkled and instantly antiqued. It is up to you how aged your quilt becomes. Be ready to explain to your friends just what happened to your quilt and that you wanted it to be all spotted.

For larger quilts, use a large pan or bucket and ten to twelve tea bags. Steep the tea in the microwave in the same manner as directed above.

Stenciled Quilt Projects

*R*efer to the stenciling directions on pages 17–22 to stencil your quilts. In addition to the materials listed for each quilt project, you will need the items listed in the master supply list below.

Master Supply List

Freezer paper

Pencil

Scissors

Cuticle scissors or craft knife
and cutting mat

Rotary cutter and cutting mat

Acrylic ruler

Sponges
(I prefer cosmetic sponges)

Stencil brushes

Paper towels

Paper plates

Iron, ironing board,
and press cloth

Black permanent pens
(I prefer Sharpie Fine Point
and Ultra Fine Point pens)

Paper

Transparent tape

Sewing machine and
general sewing supplies

Cotton or cotton-wrapped
polyester thread

Between or quilting needle
(#9 works best for me)
for hand quilting

Cotton quilting thread

Small Basket

By Vicki Garnas, 12½" x 12½".

Baskets of flowers were a common design element in early-American stenciled quilts.
The sawtooth border triangles on the quilt are also stenciled, not pieced.

This little basket-and-flowers quilt is a perfect place to begin learning the stenciling techniques used in the larger quilts. The stenciling is as simple as the construction.

Materials

¼ yd. light-colored print for border

8½" square of light plaid for background of Basket block

15" square for backing

¼ yd. dark print for binding

15" square of batting

Materials as listed in "Master Supply List" on page 29

Acrylic craft paint in red, green, blue, and yellow

1"-wide masking tape

Cutting

From the border fabric, cut:

2 strips, 2½" x 12½"

2 strips, 2½" x 8½"

From the dark print fabric, cut:

2 strips, 2" x 42"

Stenciling

Refer to "Stenciling in the Twenty-First Century" on page 17 for basic stenciling directions.

1. Using the pattern on page 33 and three 8½" squares of freezer paper, make a 3-part basket stencil. Also make the sawtooth border stencil, using the pattern on page 32 and a 2½" x 12½" rectangle of freezer paper. Center the border pattern along the length of the freezer paper.
2. Center basket stencil 1 on the 8½" background square and fuse. Stencil the basket blue. Remove the stencil.
3. Align positioning lines of basket stencil 2 with the edges of the basket and fuse. Stencil the flowers red. Remove the stencil.

4. Align positioning lines of basket stencil 3 with the flowers and basket; fuse. Stencil the leaves green, and the flower centers yellow. Remove the stencil. Press to heat-set (page 21).
5. Center the sawtooth-border stencil on a border strip, aligning the long edge of the stencil with one long edge of the fabric and matching the centers. Fuse in place. Stencil the sawtooth border in red, stenciling all the way to the edge of the fabric. Repeat for all border strips. Press to heat-set (page 21). For the short side borders, align the ends of the strips with the marked lines on the stencil. The stencil will extend beyond the ends of the side border strips.

Assembling and Finishing the Quilt

1. Join the 8½"-long stenciled border strips to the sides of the basket square, matching the ends. Press the seams toward the borders. Join the 12½"-long stenciled border strips to the top and bottom edges of the quilt, matching the ends. Press the seams toward the borders.

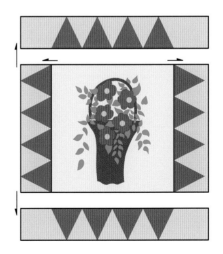

2. Referring to the project photo, use a black Sharpie Ultra Fine Point pen to outline the basket, leaves, and flowers. Draw in the vines, connecting the leaves. Draw the vein lines on the leaves and draw in the lines around the flower centers.

3. Using a dashed line, outline the triangles on the border.

4. Layer the quilt top with batting and backing; baste. Quilt around the outer edges of the Basket block next to the edge of the border. Quilt around the flowers, flower centers, and basket.

5. Quilt a diamond pattern across the Basket block, skipping over the stenciled areas. Use 1"-wide masking tape as a guide and refer to "Quilting" on page 25. Outline-quilt around the edges of the sawtooth border design.

6. Bind the edges of the quilt and add a label.

7. Give the quilt an aged appearance if desired, following "Aging Your Quilt" on page 27.

Small Basket
Sawtooth Border Stencil 1
Actual size

Stencil 1

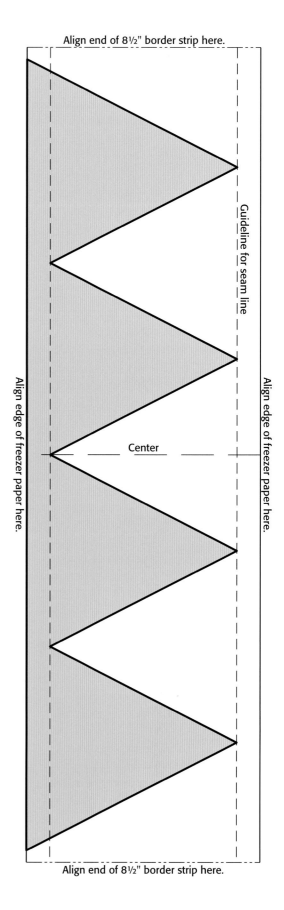

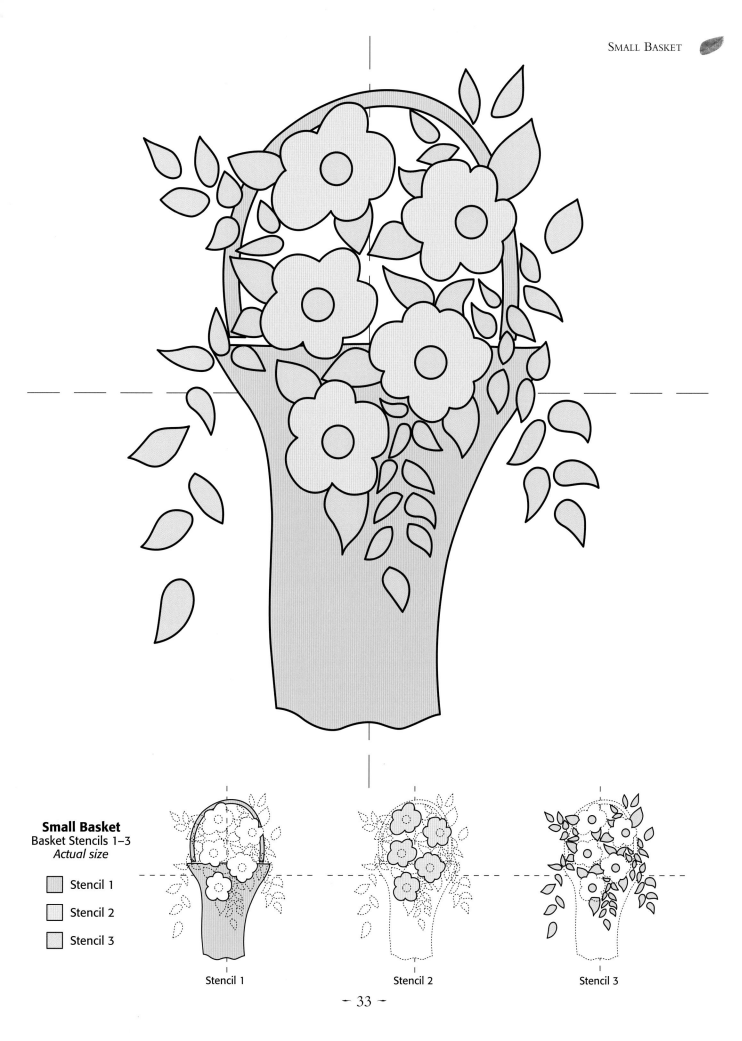

Small Basket
Basket Stencils 1–3
Actual size

Stencil 1
Stencil 2
Stencil 3

Stencil 1   Stencil 2   Stencil 3

Posy Wreath

By Vicki Garnas, 29" x 29".

This quilt is based on a traditional appliqué pattern called Bridal Wreath.

The Bridal Wreath pattern is an American classic. This quilt has a contemporary feel due to the pattern of some of the fabrics, but the quilt colors and design resemble those used around 1830. The mustard yellow fabric is in the color range available to quilters from 1820–40; the red used in the sashing and binding is also true to the era.

Materials

4 fat quarters or ⅝ yd. total of mustard prints for border

⅜ yd. each of 1 or 2 white small-scale prints for background

¼ yd. red print for sashing

1 yd. fabric for backing

⅜ yd. red stripe for binding

1 yd. batting

Materials as listed in "Master Supply List" on page 29

Acrylic craft paint in red, green, and gold

1½"-wide masking tape

Cutting

From the white small-scale print, cut:

Four 8½" squares

From the red print, cut:

3 strips, 2" x 42"; crosscut strips into a total of 2 strips, 2" x 8½"; 3 strips, 2" x 18"; and 2 strips, 2" x 21".

From the mustard prints, cut:

A total of 8 lengthwise strips, 4½" wide, cutting at least 1 strip from each fabric

From the red stripe, cut:

4 strips, 2" x 42"

Stenciling the Blocks

Refer to "Stenciling in the Twenty-First Century" on page 17 for basic stenciling directions.

1. Using the pattern on page 38, make a 2-part Posy Wreath stencil, using two 8½" squares of freezer paper. Save the flower-center cutouts from wreath stencil 1.

2. Align wreath stencil 1 on an 8½" background square and fuse. Stencil the wreath vines and leaves green and the flower centers gold. Remove the stencil.

3. Align positioning lines of wreath stencil 2 with the edges of the vines and leaves; fuse. Align the center cutouts over the stenciled flower centers and fuse. Stencil the posies red. Remove the stencil and cutouts.

4. Press to heat-set (page 21). Make 4.

Assembling the Quilt

1. Sew 2 Posy Wreath blocks and one 2" x 8½" sashing strip together as shown. Repeat for the second pair of Posy Wreath blocks.

Make 2.

2. Join the 2 wreath pairs with a 2" x 18" sashing strip. Sew the remaining 2" x 18" sashing strips to the side edges of the 4-block unit. Press the seams toward the sashing.

3. Sew the 2" x 21" sashing strips to the top and bottom edges of the quilt top. Press the seams toward the sashing.

4. Trim the mustard print strips to various lengths. Sew the strips end to end in a random order to make 2 strips about the same length. Press the seams open.

5. Referring to "Borders" on page 23, measure and trim the border strips and sew them to the side edges of the quilt top first, and then to the top and bottom edges.

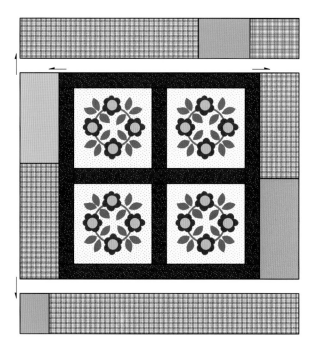

Stenciling the Borders

Refer to "Stenciling in the Twenty-First Century" on page 17 for basic stenciling directions.

1. Using the pattern on page 39 and two 4½" x 14" strips of freezer paper, make a 2-part border stencil. Center the border pattern along the length of the freezer-paper strips. Save the flower-center cutouts from stencil 1.

2. Also make a 2-part border corner stencil, using the pattern on page 40 and two 4½" squares of freezer paper. Save the flower-center cutout from border corner stencil 1.

3. Mark the center of the border on each side with a pin. Position the center line of border stencil 1 at the center pin mark of the border on one side of the quilt and fuse. Stencil the vines and leaves green and the flower centers gold. Remove the stencil.

4. Align positioning lines of border stencil 2 with the edges of the vines and leaves; fuse. Align the center cutouts over the stenciled flower centers and fuse. Stencil the posies red. Remove the stencil and cutouts. Repeat the border stenciling on the remaining 3 sides of the quilt. Press to heat-set (page 21).

5. Position border corner stencil 1 in one corner of the quilt, aligning outside edges and aligning the corner of the sashing with the stencil inside corner; fuse. Stencil the leaves green and the flower center gold. Remove the stencil.

6. Align positioning lines of border corner stencil 2 with the edges of the leaves, and the corner of the sashing with the stencil inside corner; fuse. Align the flower-center cutout over the stenciled flower center and fuse. Stencil the posy red. Remove the stencil and cutout. Repeat at the remaining 3 corners of the quilt. Press the border to heat-set.

Finishing

1. Referring to the project photo and the detail below, use a Sharpie Ultra Fine Point pen to outline the flowers, leaves, vines, and posy centers with a fine line. Draw center vein lines on the leaves.

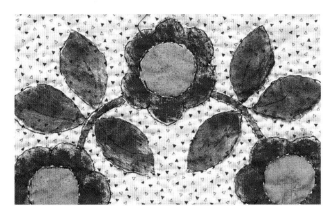

Outline stenciled motifs and add details with a black pen. Draw vein lines on leaves as shown.

2. Layer the quilt top with batting and backing; baste. Quilt in the ditch of the seam lines of the blocks and inner edge of the border.

3. Quilt a diamond pattern across the quilt, skipping over the stenciled areas. Use 1½"-wide masking tape as a guide and refer to "Quilting" on page 25.

4. Bind the edges of the quilt and add a label.

5. Although my quilt was not aged much, you can give your quilt an aged appearance if desired by following "Aging Your Quilt" on page 27.

Posy Wreath
Wreath Stencils 1–2
Actual size

Stencil 1

Stencil 2

Stencil 1

Stencil 2

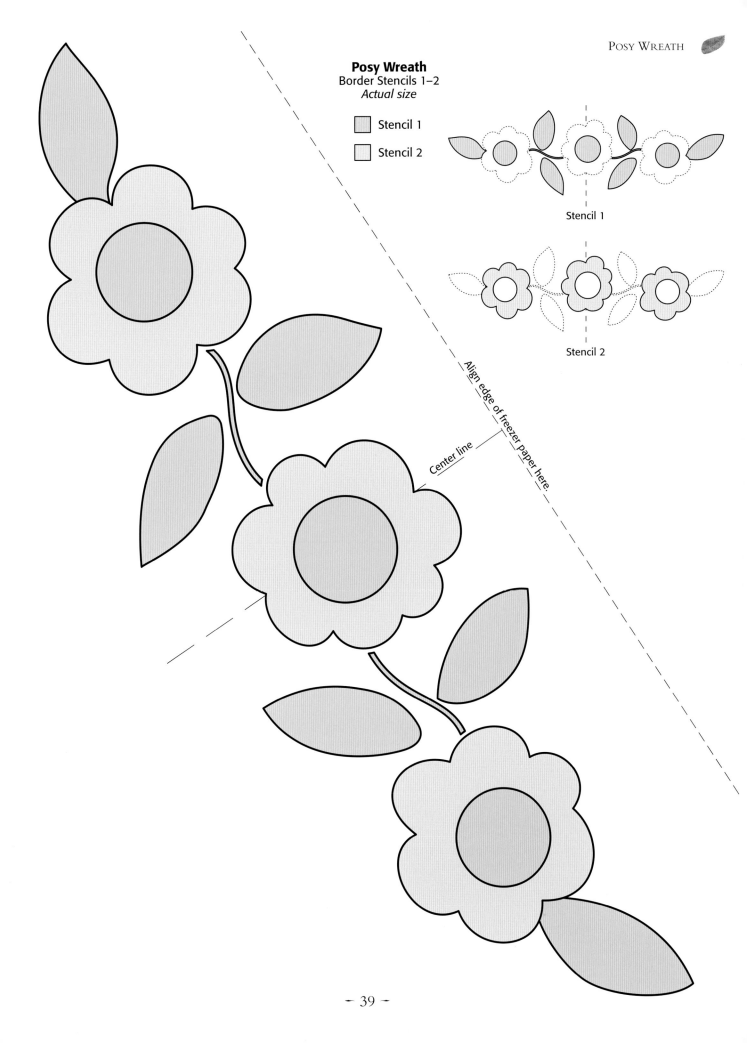

Posy Wreath
Border Stencils 1–2
Actual size

☐ Stencil 1

☐ Stencil 2

Stencil 1

Stencil 2

Align edge of freezer paper here.

Center line

Inside corner

Outside edge

Outside edge

Posy Wreath
Border Corner Stencils 1–2
Actual size

Stencil 1

Stencil 2

Stencil 1   Stencil 2

Nine Patch and Roses

By Vicki Garnas, 47¾" x 47¾".

This stenciled quilt is based on the quilt design by Mary Ann Hoyt on page 13.

Flowers were popular motifs for quilting and stenciling in the nineteenth century, and the rose was one of the most popular. "Nine Patch and Roses" is a replica of a stenciled and pieced quilt made by Mary Ann Hoyt in 1834. It is now in the collection of the Winterthur Museum in Delaware. I omitted my usual pen-work outlines around the rose design and left wider spaces between the painted parts to imitate the design details of the antique stenciled quilts. This is an easy project to piece and stencil.

Materials

2¼ yds. muslin for stenciled blocks, Nine Patch blocks, and binding

1 yd. total print scraps for Nine Patch blocks★

3 yds. fabric for backing

54" square of batting

Materials as listed in "Master Supply List" on page 29

Acrylic craft paint in rose, red, and green

Kitchen sponge cut into 1" chunks

1½"-wide masking tape

★ *Choose several different tones and patterns. I chose fabrics in red, gold, green, brown, and gray.*

Cutting

From the muslin, cut:

Twenty-four 7¼" squares

8 strips, 2¾" x 42"

6 strips, 2" x 42"

From the print scraps, cut:

10 strips, 2¾" x 42"

Stenciling the Rose Blocks

Refer to "Stenciling in the Twenty-First Century" on page 17 for basic stenciling directions.

1. Using the pattern on page 44, make a 2-part rose stencil, using two 7¼" squares of freezer paper.

Each stencil pattern can be used up to 6 times; therefore, you will need to make the 2-part stencil 4 times to stencil 24 blocks.

2. Align rose stencil 1 on a muslin square and fuse. Stencil the leaves and stems green using a kitchen sponge. This sponge will leave the paint spotty, but this is okay. Remove the stencil.

3. Align positioning lines of rose stencil 2 with the edges of the stems and leaves; fuse. Stencil 2 roses and bud with rose paint; then lightly go over them in red to give a faded, worn look to the motifs. Remove the stencil. Press to heat-set (page 21). Make 24.

Assembling the Nine Patch Blocks

You will need 25 Nine Patch blocks for this quilt. The instructions below are for 25 blocks, but I always make extra and then choose the best of the group. I chose to make several of my Nine Patch blocks using just one print per block. If you wish to do this, you will need to cut additional strips of fabric and use the same print in both your A and B strip sets.

1. Join the 2¾"-wide print strips to the 2¾"-wide muslin strips as shown to make 4 of strip set A and 2 of strip set B. From strip set A, cut 50 segments, 2¾" wide. From strip set B, cut 25 segments, 2¾" wide.

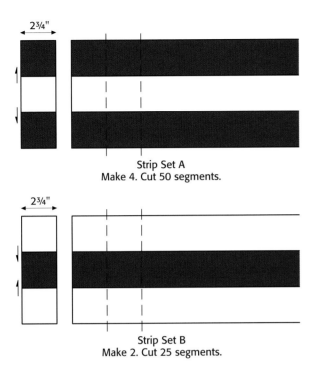

Strip Set A
Make 4. Cut 50 segments.

Strip Set B
Make 2. Cut 25 segments.

2. Join the segments from step 1 as shown to make a Nine Patch block.

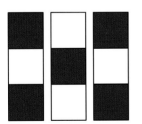 

Nine Patch Block
Make 25.

Assembling and Finishing the Quilt

1. Arrange the blocks into 7 rows of 7 blocks each, alternating Rose and Nine Patch blocks as shown. Sew the blocks together in horizontal rows.

2. Sew the rows together. Piece the backing fabric as necessary. Layer the quilt top with batting and backing; baste.

3. Quilt around the roses, stems, leaves, and buds and through the bridges (white spaces) of the roses.

4. Quilt a diamond pattern across the quilt, skipping over the stenciled areas. Use 1½"-wide masking tape as a guide and refer to "Quilting" on page 25.

5. Bind the edges of the quilt with the 2"-wide muslin strips and add a label.

6. Give the quilt an aged appearance if desired, following "Aging Your Quilt" on page 27.

Nine Patch and Roses
Stencils 1–2
Actual size

Stencil 1

Stencil 2

Stencil 1

Stencil 2

Pot of Flowers Medallion

By Vicki Garnas, 35½" x 35½".

This quilt is based on those made during the nineteenth century with an appliquéd center and pieced borders.

Medallion quilts with a central square and several borders were made during the early part of the nineteenth century in America. A pot of flowers was traditional as the center square. The earliest quilts had a cutout and appliquéd motif of flowers and birds with butterflies. For this medallion quilt, I designed a simple stenciled pot of flowers for an easy center square, then framed it with a striped inner border, a pieced middle border, and a fun stenciled outer border. I would never attempt to appliqué the swirling vine and berries, but stenciling them is easy.

Materials

10 fat quarters or ¾ yd. total of different dark and medium prints for pieced middle border and corner squares

1 yd. muslin for center square and borders

6 fat quarters or ⅜ yd. total of different light prints for pieced middle border and corner squares

¼ yd. green stripe for inner border

1¼ yds. fabric for backing

⅜ yd. red print for binding

40" square of batting

Materials as listed in "Master Supply List" on page 29

Acrylic craft paints in red, moss green, bright green, gold, and blue

¾"-wide masking tape

Cutting

From the muslin, cut:

One 14½" square

4 strips, 6" x 24½"

From the green stripe, cut:

2 strips, 1½" x 14½"

2 strips, 1½" x 16½"

From the dark and medium prints, cut:

Twenty 4¼" squares; cut squares twice diagonally to yield 80 triangles.

From the light prints, cut:

Twenty 3¼" squares

From the desired light, medium, and dark prints for corner squares, cut:

Four 3¼" squares

Eight 3½" squares, 2 from each of 4 fabrics; cut squares in half once diagonally to yield 16 triangles.

Four 4¼" squares; cut squares twice diagonally to yield 16 triangles.

From the red print, cut:

5 strips, 2" x 42"

Stenciling

Refer to "Stenciling in the Twenty-First Century" on page 17 for basic stenciling directions.

1. Enlarge the patterns on pages 49–50 for the center block and border on a photocopy machine, as indicated on the patterns. Then make master patterns for the center block and border, referring to "The Master Pattern" on page 20.

2. Using the master patterns created in step 1, make a 3-part stencil for the center block using three 14½" squares of freezer paper. Also make a 3-part stencil for the border, using three 6" x 24½" strips of freezer paper.

3. Center stencil 1 for the center block on the muslin square; fuse. Stencil the stems moss green. Remove the stencil.

4. Center stencil 2 on the muslin square, aligning the positioning lines with the stenciled stems; fuse. Referring to the project photo, stencil the large center flower and petaled flowers red, and the tulips and bell flowers blue. Add a little blue around the outer edges of the large center flower for shadow. Remove the stencil.

5. Center stencil 3 on the muslin square, aligning the positioning lines with the edges if the stenciled design; fuse. Stencil the centers of the petaled flowers gold. Stencil the vase gold, lightly adding a little blue at the edges for shadow (see photo). Stencil the leaves moss green. Remove the stencil. Press to heat-set (page 21).

6. Fold the muslin strips in half to find the centers; mark. Align border stencil 1 with the edge of a muslin strip, matching the centers; fuse. Stencil the tulips gold, the berries red, and the center flower blue. Remove the stencil.

7. Align positioning lines of border stencil 2 with the edges of the flowers and berries; fuse. Stencil the leaves, vines, and tulip bases bright green and the center flower red. Remove the stencil.

8. Align positioning lines of border stencil 3 with the edges of the stenciled design; fuse. Stencil the flower center gold and the leaves moss green. Remove the stencil.

9. Stencil all 4 border strips in the same manner. Press to heat-set (page 21).

Pen Work

1. Referring to the photo on page 45 and the detail below, use a black Sharpie Fine Point pen to outline the stenciled vase, stems, and flowers on the center square. Draw in the vein lines on the leaves. Draw in the details of the bellflower centers and draw lines connecting the bellflowers to the stems.

2. Outline the border flowers, leaves, stems, berries, and flower centers. Draw in the vein lines on the leaves.

Assembling the Quilt

The pieced middle border is constructed from 4" finished Square-in-a-Square blocks. Use the dark and medium prints for the triangles of the blocks and the light prints for the centers. Using 4 different fabrics for the 4 triangles of the blocks gives them a scrappy look. You will need a total of 20 Square-in-a-Square blocks for the pieced border. I usually make more so I can play with the placement of the colors and the blocks.

1. Join the 1½" x 14½" green stripe border strips to the sides of the stenciled center block. Press the seams toward the borders.

2. Join the 1½" x 16½" border strips to the top and bottom of the stenciled center block. Press the seams toward the borders.

3. For the middle border, join triangles of different dark and/or medium prints to opposite sides of a 3¼" light print square. Press the seams toward the triangles. Join 2 different dark and/or medium print triangles to the remaining 2 sides of the square. Press the seams toward the triangles. Trim to 4½" square to complete a Square-in-a-Square block.

Square-in-a-Square Block
Make 20.

4. Join 4 Square-in-a-Square blocks to make a side border strip. Repeat to make a second side border strip. Border strips should measure 16½" long. If the border is a bit too long or too short, adjust the seams between blocks as necessary.

5. Join 6 Square-in-a-Square blocks to make each of the top and bottom border strips. The strips should measure 24½" long.

6. Join the 16½"-long pieced border strips to the sides of the quilt top. Press the seams toward the borders. Join the 24½"-long strips to the top and bottom of the quilt top. Press the seams toward the borders.

7. Make 4 Square-in-a-Square blocks as in step 3, using 4 triangles from the same fabric to border each of the 3¼" squares.

8. Join 3½" triangles cut from the same fabric to opposite sides of the Square-in-a-Square block. Press the seams toward the triangles. Join matching triangles to the remaining sides of the square to make a corner square. Trim the corner square to 6" square.

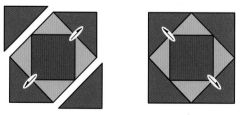

Make 4.

9. Join the stenciled border strips to the side edges of the quilt top, matching the center of the borders to the center of the quilt top at the edges. Press the seams toward the stenciled border.

10. Join the corner squares to each end of the remaining stenciled borders. Press the seams toward the border strips. Join the borders to the top and bottom of the quilt top, matching the centers and seams. Press the seams toward the stenciled border.

Finishing

1. Layer the quilt top with batting and backing; baste. Quilt around the vase and flower designs in the center square. Quilt along the seams of the inner border and between the middle and outer border.

2. Quilt a diamond pattern across the center block of the quilt, skipping over the stenciled areas. Use ¾"-wide masking tape as a guide and refer to "Quilting" on page 25.

3. Quilt along the seam lines between the Square-in-a-Square blocks of the middle border, and outline quilt around the squares in each block. Quilt through the middle of the light squares in the pieced border in both directions.

4. Quilt around the stenciled border design and the centers of the flowers.

5. Bind the edges of the quilt and add a label.

6. Give the quilt an aged appearance if desired, following "Aging Your Quilt" on page 27.

Pot of Flowers Medallion
Center Block Stencils 1–3
Enlarge pattern 150 percent.

Stencil 1

Stencil 2

Stencil 3

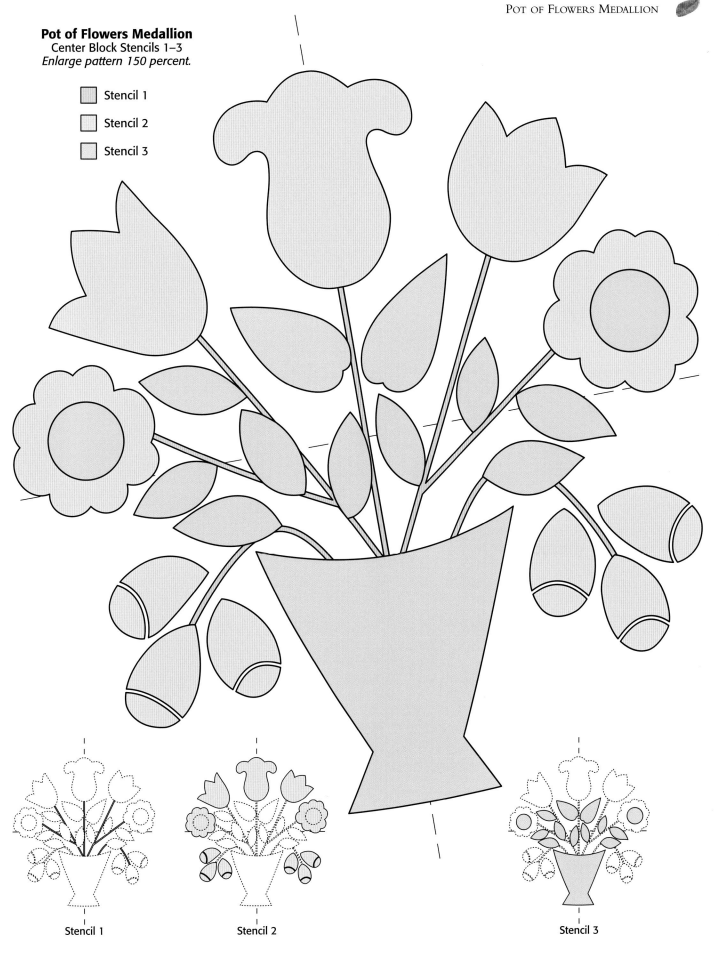

Stencil 1

Stencil 2

Stencil 3

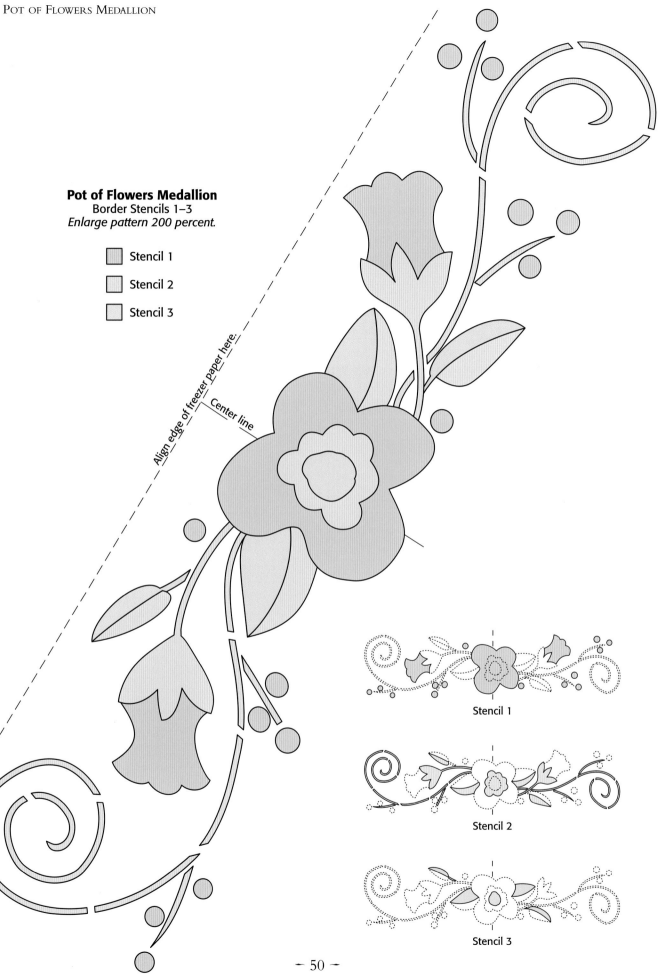

Pot of Flowers Medallion
Border Stencils 1–3
Enlarge pattern 200 percent.

Stencil 1

Stencil 2

Stencil 3

Align edge of freezer paper here.

Center line

Stencil 1

Stencil 2

Stencil 3

Red and Green Crib Quilt

By Vicki Garnas, 38" x 25".

This stenciled whole-cloth quilt of muslin is based on an 1840 appliquéd crib quilt.

This little whole-cloth quilt was inspired by a picture in *Glorious American Quilts.* I fell in love with the "Basket of Flowers with Vine Border Appliqué Crib Quilt," c.1850–60, on page 182. The quirkiness of the fat vine border and flowers flowing from the basket made me want to make one of my own with stencils and paint.

Materials

1¼ yd. muslin for background and binding

1¼ yd. fabric for backing

29" x 42" piece of batting

Materials as listed in "Master Supply List" on page 29

Acrylic craft paint in red, gold, rose, and green

1½"-wide masking tape

Cutting

From the muslin, cut:

1 rectangle, 28" x 41"

4 strips, 2" x 42"

Stenciling

Refer to "Stenciling in the Twenty-First Century" on page 17 for basic stenciling directions.

1. Enlarge the pattern on pages 54–55 on a photocopy machine as indicated on the pattern. Then make a master pattern referring to "The Master Pattern" on page 20, using a 28" x 41" piece of paper.

2. Using the master pattern created in step 1, make a 3-part stencil, using three 28" x 41" pieces of freezer paper. For stencil 1, save the center circle cutouts and the inner ring of petal cutouts from the double-petaled flowers.

3. Center stencil 1 onto the muslin rectangle; fuse. Position the inner ring of petal cutouts and the circle cutouts in the flower openings. Then, without disturbing the circle cutouts, remove and save for step 4 the inner ring of petal cutouts. Fuse the circle cutouts in place. Stencil the stems, leaves, and vine border green. Using rose, stencil the inner ring of the double-petaled flowers and the center tulip petals. Remove the stencil. Connect the vine and stems by filling in the white spaces, using green paint and a small brush.

4. Place stencil 2 over the muslin, aligning the positioning lines with the edges of the stenciled design; fuse. Position the inner ring of petal cutouts over the stenciled areas of the double-petaled flowers, aligning edges; fuse. Stencil the remaining flower petals and the buds red. Check to make sure all areas are stenciled. Remove the stencil and the inner ring of petal and circle cutouts.

5. Place stencil 3 over the muslin, aligning the positioning lines with the edges of the stenciled design; fuse. Stencil the basket and flower centers gold. Remove the stencil.

6. Press to heat-set (page 21).

Pen Work

Referring to the project photo on page 51 and the detail below, use a black Sharpie Ultra Fine Point pen to outline the basket design with dashed lines. Outline the stems, leaves, flowers, and buds with dashed lines and add vein lines to the leaves.

Finishing

1. Trim the edges of the quilt top to measure 38" x 25" and check that corners are square. Retrim as necessary.

2. Layer the quilt top with batting and backing; baste. Outline-quilt around the basket, flowers, stems, and leaves. Add quilted designs such as flowers, leaves, and hearts to the background in open areas.

3. Quilt a diamond pattern across the quilt, skipping over the stenciled areas. Use 1½"-wide masking tape as a guide and refer to "Quilting" on page 25.

4. Bind the edges of the quilt and add a label.

5. Give the quilt an aged appearance if desired, following "Aging Your Quilt" on page 27.

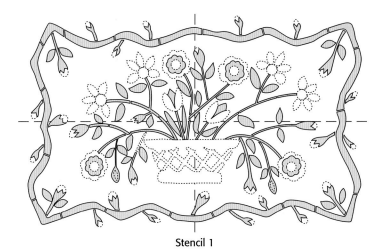

Stencil 1

Stencil 2

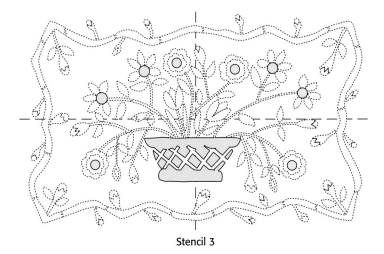

Stencil 3

Connect to right half on page 55.

**Red and Green Crib Quilt
Left Half**
Stencils 1–3
Enlarge pattern 250 percent.

Stencil 1

Stencil 2

Stencil 3

Connect to left half on page 54.

Red and Green Crib Quilt
Right Half
Stencils 1–3
Enlarge pattern 250 percent.

Stencil 1

Stencil 2

Stencil 3

Theorem Stenciled Baskets

By Vicki Garnas, 40½" x 40½".

This muslin quilt was stenciled to resemble intricate appliquéd basket quilts.
The baskets are similar to a theorem-stenciled still life made around 1820–30.

The American stenciled quilts made during the nineteenth century share roots in two areas of American folk art: quilting and stenciling. This quilt was inspired by an appliqué quilt (c. 1840) with filled baskets and two appliquéd borders. I would not attempt to re-create the quilt in appliqué, but stenciling it was fun. The baskets and their contents remind me of the theorem pictures young ladies made during the 1830s. These stencils are based on those still-life images and the basket quilt from the same time period. The stenciling on this muslin quilt is not difficult, but there is a lot of it. Take it step by step; enjoy the process and the completed quilt.

Materials

2½ yds. muslin for block backgrounds, sashing, borders, and binding

2½ yds. fabric for backing

44" square of batting

Materials as listed in "Master Supply List" on page 29

Acrylic paint in red, medium green, dark green, brown, light blue, dark blue, rose, gold, light yellow, and purple

1½"-wide masking tape

Cutting

From the muslin, cut:

Four 12" squares

6 strips, 2½" x 42"; crosscut strips into 2 strips, 2½" x 12"; 3 strips, 2½" x 25½"; and 2 strips, 2½" x 29½"

5 strips, 6" x 42"

5 strips, 2" x 42"

Stenciling the Blocks

Refer to "Stenciling in the Twenty-First Century" on page 17 for basic stenciling directions.

1. Enlarge the patterns on pages 61–64 for each of the 4 basket blocks (grape, apple, bird, and tulip) on a photocopy machine as indicated on the patterns. Then make a master pattern for each, referring to "The Master Pattern" on page 20.

2. Using the master patterns created in step 1, make 3-part stencils for the grape and apple baskets and 2-part stencils for the bird and tulip baskets, using 12" x 12" squares of freezer paper.

Grape Basket

1. Center stencil 1 of the grape basket on a 12" background square; fuse. Referring to the project photo, stencil the basket sections dark blue, the cherries rose, and the grapes purple. Stencil the cherry leaves medium green and the remaining leaves dark green. Remove the stencil.

2. Align positioning lines of stencil 2 with the edges of the stenciled design; fuse. Stencil the basket section gold, the left apple red, the right apple medium green, and the strawberries red. Remove the stencil.

3. Align positioning lines of stencil 3 with the edges of the basket and fruit; fuse. Stencil the grapes purple. Remove the stencil.

Apple Basket

1. Center stencil 1 of the apple basket on a 12" background square; fuse. Referring to the project photo, stencil the basket sections gold, the apple green, and the flower clusters light yellow. Remove the stencil.

2. Align positioning lines of stencil 2 with the edges of the basket, apple, and flowers; fuse. Stencil the basket section and the apple red and the leaves medium green. Remove the stencil.

3. Align positioning lines of stencil 3 with the edges of the stenciled design; fuse. Stencil the leaves and stems dark green. Remove the stencil.

Bird Basket

1. Center stencil 1 of the bird basket on a 12" background square; fuse. Referring to the project photo, stencil the basket gold, the bird red, and the leaves dark green. Remove the stencil.

2. Align positioning lines of stencil 2 with the edges of the basket and bird and leaves; fuse. Stencil the bird wing, beak, and stems brown, the basket stripes and flowers red, and the pears gold. Remove the stencil.

Tulip Basket

1. Center stencil 1 of the tulip basket on a 12" background square; fuse. Referring to the project photo, stencil the basket gold, the tulip light blue, 2 of the 4-petaled flowers purple, and 2 rose. Remove the stencil.

2. Align positioning lines of stencil 2 with the edges of the basket and flowers; fuse. Stencil the basket lines dark blue, the small flowers rose, and the leaves and stems dark green. Remove the stencil.

3. Using dark green paint and a small brush, fill in spaces between stems and leaves.

Pen Work

Referring to the project photo on page 56 and the detail photos below, use a Sharpie Fine Point pen to outline the baskets, fruit, leaves, and bird; and draw details on the fruit, flowers, and leaves.

On the grape basket, add vein lines to the leaves. Add stems to the cherries. Draw lines to separate grapes at the top of the cluster.

On the apple basket, add vein lines to the leaves.

On the bird basket, make a dot for the bird's eye, outline wing, and add feet. Add stems and vein lines to the leaves.

On the tulip basket, mark centers for the petaled flowers and add stems to the remaining leaves. Add vein lines to the leaves.

Assembling the Quilt

The sashing and border designs are stenciled after the quilt top is assembled.

1. Join pairs of basket blocks and 2½" x 12" sashing strips together as shown.

2. Join the grape-apple unit to the bird-tulip unit with a 2½" x 25½" sashing strip.

3. Join 2½" x 25½" inner-border strips to opposite sides of the 4-basket unit. Join 2½" x 29½" inner-border strips to the top and bottom of the 4-basket unit.

Stenciling the Berry Vine Sashing and the Inner Borders

Refer to "Stenciling in the Twenty-First Century" on page 17 for basic stenciling directions.

1. Using the pattern on page 65, make a 2-part stencil for the berry vine, using two 2½" x 12" strips of freezer paper. Center the stencil along the length of each piece of freezer paper.

Each stencil can be used up to 6 times. Make additional 2-part stencils for the berry vine as necessary to stencil the sashing and inner border.

2. Align berry vine stencil 1, berries pointing up, with the 2½" x 12" sashing strip between the grape and apple blocks; fuse. Stencil the vines dark green and the berries rose. Remove the stencil. Repeat on the sashing strip between the bird and tulip blocks, except position the stencil with the berries pointing down.

3. Align positioning lines of berry stencil 2 with the edges of the berries and vines; fuse. Stencil the leaves and berry tops green. Remove the stencil. Repeat on the remaining 2½" x 12" sashing strip.

4. Position berry stencil 1, berries pointing left, with one end of the long center sashing strip; fuse. Stencil the vines dark green and the berries rose. Remove the stencil and reposition it along the strip so that the vine on the stencil is about ¼" from the end of the stenciled vine. Stencil the vines dark green and berries rose. Continue in this manner until the stenciling reaches the opposite end of the sashing strip. Remove the stencil.

5. Stencil the long center sashing strip with berry stencil 2 in the same manner as for the short sashing strips. Stencil the berry vine on each side of the inner border, stopping to rotate the stencil at the midpoint of each side so that the berries point away from the center, toward the ends of the strips on each side (see project photo).

Assembling and Stenciling the Outer Border

Refer to "Stenciling in the Twenty-First Century" on page 17 for basic stenciling directions.

1. Referring to "Borders" on page 23, and using the 6" x 42" outer-border strips, measure and trim, and sew them to the side edges of the quilt top, and then to the top and bottom edges.

2. Using the patterns on pages 66–69, make a master pattern for the outer border, referring to "The Master Pattern" on page 20.

3. Using the master pattern created in step 2, make a 2-part stencil for the outer border, using two 6" x 33" strips of freezer paper.

4. Align border stencil 1 along one side of the border with the corner portion of the stencil aligned with a corner of the quilt; fuse. Stencil the vines dark green and the flowers gold. Remove the stencil. Repeat the stenciling process on the remaining 3 sides of the outer border, aligning the stencil with the previously stenciled design in each corner.

5. Align border stencil 2 along one side of the border, aligning positioning lines of stencil with the edges of the stenciled designs. Stencil the leaves dark green and the flower centers red. Remove the stencil. Repeat the stenciling process on the remaining 3 sides of the outer border.

Finishing

1. Press the entire quilt top to heat-set (page 21). Referring to the project photo on page 56 and the detail below, use a Sharpie Ultra Fine Point pen to outline the vines, leaves, and flowers. Draw in the stems and vein lines on the leaves. Draw in the petals on the flowers. The inner berry border is not outlined with pen work.

2. Piece the backing fabric as necessary. Layer the quilt top with batting and backing; baste. Quilt around the baskets, fruit, and flowers. Quilt at the seams of the blocks and sashings. Quilt along the vines in the berry sashings. Quilt around the border vines, leaves, and flowers.

3. Quilt a diamond pattern across the quilt, skipping over the stenciled areas. Use 1½"-wide masking tape as a guide and refer to "Quilting" on page 25.

4. Bind the edges of the quilt and add a label.

5. Give the quilt an aged appearance if desired, following "Aging Your Quilt" on page 27.

Theorem Stenciled Baskets
Grape Basket Stencils 1–3
Enlarge pattern 133 percent.

◼ Stencil 1

◻ Stencil 2

▢ Stencil 3

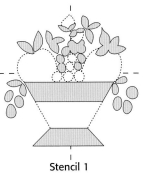

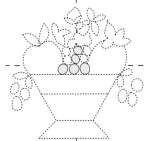

Stencil 1   Stencil 2   Stencil 3

Theorem Stenciled Baskets
Apple Basket Stencils 1–3
Enlarge pattern 133 percent.

Stencil 1

Stencil 2

Stencil 3

Stencil 1

Stencil 2

Stencil 3

Theorem Stenciled Baskets
Bird Basket Stencils 1–2
Enlarge pattern 133 percent.

Stencil 1

Stencil 2

Stencil 1

Stencil 2

Theorem Stenciled Baskets
Tulip Basket Stencils 1–2
Enlarge pattern 133 percent.

Stencil 1

Stencil 2

Stencil 1

Stencil 2

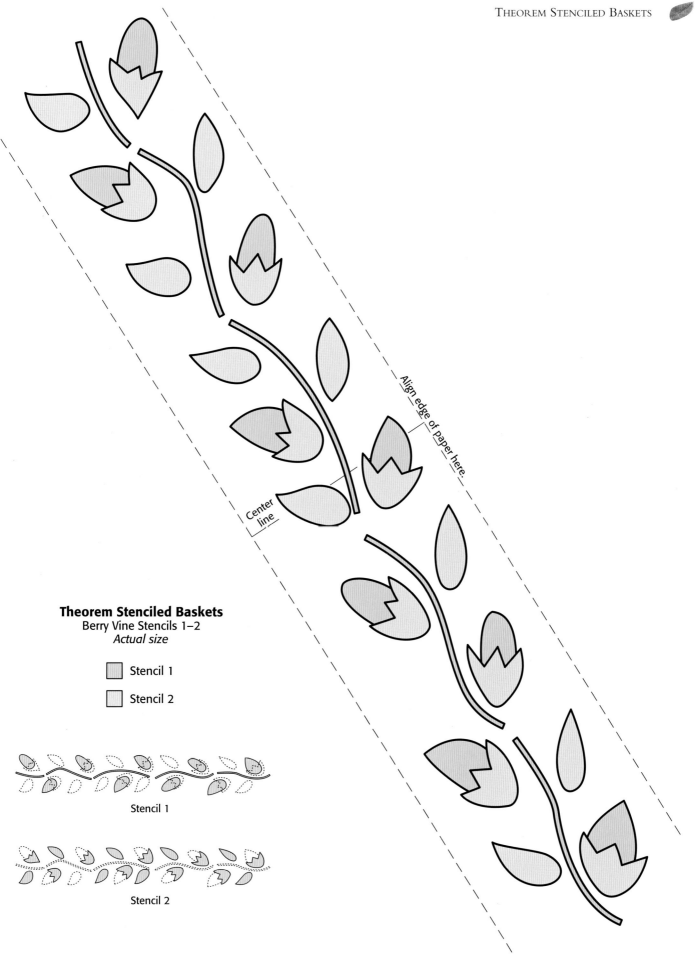

Theorem Stenciled Baskets
Berry Vine Stencils 1–2
Actual size

Stencil 1

Stencil 2

Stencil 1

Stencil 2

Align edge of paper here.

Center line

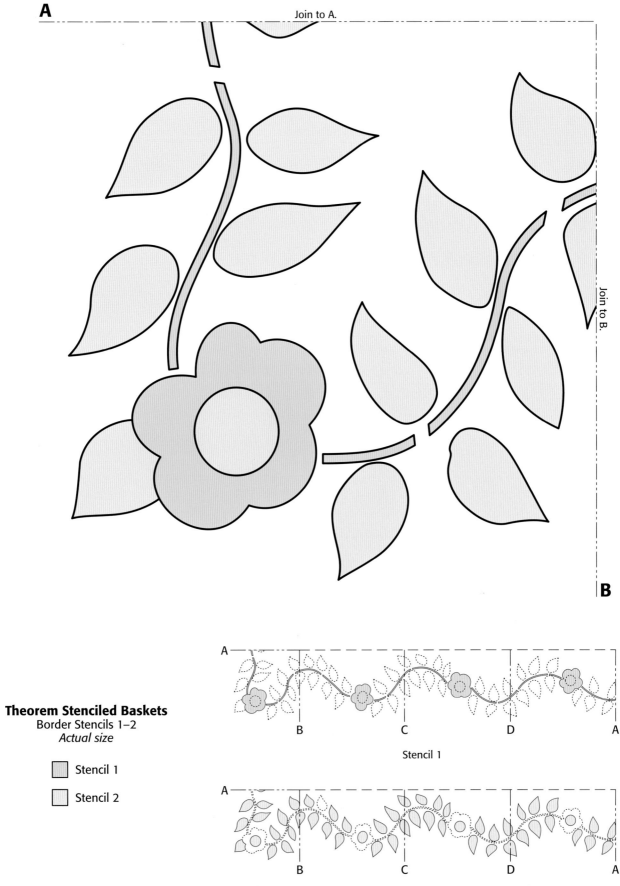

A

Join to A.

Join to B.

B

Theorem Stenciled Baskets
Border Stencils 1–2
Actual size

Stencil 1

Stencil 2

Stencil 1

Stencil 2

Join to B.

B

Theorem Stenciled Baskets
Border Stencils 1–2
Actual size

Stencil 1

Stencil 2

Align edge of paper here.

C

Join to C.

Join to C.

C

Theorem Stenciled Baskets
Border Stencils 1–2
Actual size

Stencil 1

Stencil 2

Align edge of paper here.

Join to D.

D

Join to D.

D

Theorem Stenciled Baskets
Border Stencils 1–2
Actual size

Stencil 1

Stencil 2

Join to A.

A

Tulip and Posy Four Patch

By Vicki Garnas, 38½" x 38½".

This quilt has easy-to-stencil large floral designs in the blocks. The same motifs are repeated in the borders with added curvy vines and circle berries.

Large appliquéd four-block quilts were popular during the mid 1900s. This stenciled quilt is roughly based on those quilts, repeating the same block in two colorways and adding a coordinating floral border. A small print was used for the background to add more visual texture to the quilt. The stenciled design along the border is an elongated version of the stenciled border design used for the "Pot of Flowers Medallion" stenciled quilt on page 45. Once the stencils are cut, the quilt is simple to make.

Materials

1⅝ yds. light small-scale print for background

2½ yds. for backing

⅜ yd. light small-scale print for binding

43" square of batting

Materials as listed in "Master Supply List" on page 29

Acrylic craft paint in red, blue, light green, dark green, and gold

1½"-wide masking tape

Cutting

From the background print, cut:

Four 14" squares

4 strips, 6" x 42"

From the binding print, cut:

4 strips, 2" x 42"

Stenciling the Blocks

Refer to "Stenciling in the Twenty-First Century" on page 17 for basic stenciling directions.

1. Enlarge the block pattern on page 74 on a photocopy machine as indicated on the pattern. Then make a master pattern for the block, referring to "The Master Pattern" on page 20.

2. Using the master pattern created in step 1, make a 2-part stencil for the block, using two 14" squares of freezer paper. Be sure to include the dashed center lines on your stencils. For stencil 1, save the center circle cutouts and the inner ring of petal cutouts from the double-petaled flowers.

3. Center block stencil 1 on the background square; fuse. Position the inner ring of petal cutout and the circle cutout in the center flower opening. Then, without disturbing the circle cutout, remove and save the inner ring of petal cutout for step 4. Fuse the circle cutout in place. Stencil the leaves and stems dark green and the inner ring of the double-petaled flower blue. Remove the stencil and center circle cutout.

4. Center block stencil 2 on the background square, aligning positioning lines of stencil with the edges of the stenciled design; fuse. Position the inner ring of petal cutout over the stenciled area of the double-petaled flower, aligning edges; fuse. Stencil the leaves light green, tulips blue, outer ring of double-petaled flowers red, and center circle gold. Remove the stencil and inner ring of petal cutout.

5. Stencil a second background square in the same manner. Stencil 2 more background squares using the same stencils, but stencil the tulips red and stencil the outer ring of the double-petaled flowers blue, the inner ring gold, and the center red (see photo). Press to heat-set (page 21).

Assembling the Quilt

1. Sew 4 tulip and posy blocks together as shown, rotating blocks for desired placement.
2. Referring to "Borders" on page 23, and using the 6" x 42" border strips, measure and trim, and sew them to the side edges of the quilt top, and then to the top and bottom edges.

Stenciling the Borders

1. Enlarge the border patterns on pages 75–77 on a photocopy machine as indicated on the patterns. Then make master patterns for the borders, referring to "The Master Pattern" on page 20.
2. Using the master patterns created in step 1, make a 3-part stencil for the side border, using two 6" x 27½" strips of freezer paper. Make a 3-part stencil for the top and bottom border, using two 6" x 38½" strips of freezer paper. For stencil 1 of each border, save the center circle cutouts and the inner ring of petal cutouts from the double-petaled flowers.

3. Mark the center of each border piece along the edge on each side of the quilt. Center side border stencil 1 along the length of a short side border strip, placing the long edge of the stencil at the border seam; fuse. Position the inner ring of petal cutout and the circle cutout in the center of the flower opening. Then without disturbing the circle cutout, remove and save for step 5 the inner ring of petal cutout. Fuse the circle cutout in place. Stencil the leaves and stems dark green, and the inner ring of the double-petaled flower gold. Remove the stencil and center circle cutout.
4. Center side border stencil 2 on the border, aligning the positioning lines with the edges of the stenciled design; fuse. Stencil the leaves light green, berries gold or red, and center circle and tulips red. Remove the stencil.
5. Center side border stencil 3 on the border, aligning positioning lines with the edges of the stenciled design; fuse. Position the inner ring of petal cutout and center circle cutout over the stenciled area of the double-petaled flower, aligning edges; fuse. Stencil the outer ring of the double-petaled flower blue. Remove the stencil and cutouts. Stencil the remaining short side border in the same manner.
6. Center the top and bottom border stencil 1 along the length of a long border strip, placing the long edge of the stencil at the border seam; fuse. Position the inner ring of petal cutout and the circle cutout in the center of the flower opening. Then, without disturbing the circle cutout, remove and save for step 8 the inner ring of petal cutout. Fuse the circle in place. Stencil the leaves and stems dark green, and the inner ring of the double-petaled flower blue. Remove the stencil and center circle cutout.
7. Center top and bottom border stencil 2 on the border, aligning positioning lines with the edges of the stenciled design; fuse. Stencil the leaves light green, tulips red, and berries blue. Remove the stencil.

8. Center top and bottom stencil 3 on the border, aligning positioning lines with the edges of the stenciled design; fuse. Position the inner ring of petal cutout and center circle cutout over the stenciled area of the double-petaled flower, aligning edges, fuse. Stencil the outer ring of the double-petaled flower blue. Remove the stencil and cutouts. Stencil the remaining long border in the same manner.

9. Press borders to heat-set (page 26).

Pen Work

Referring to the photo on page 70 and the detail below, use a black Sharpie Fine Point pen to outline the flowers, stems, and leaves. Draw in veins on the leaves.

Finishing

1. Piece the backing fabric as necessary. Layer the quilt top, batting, and backing; baste. Quilt around the stenciled designs.

2. Quilt a diamond pattern across the quilt, skipping over the stenciled areas. Use 1½"-wide masking tape as a guide and refer to "Quilting" on page 25.

3. Bind the edges of the quilt and add a label.

4. Give the quilt an aged appearance if desired, following "Aging Your Quilt" on page 27.

Tulip and Posy Four Patch
Block Stencils 1–2
Enlarge pattern 200 percent.

Stencil 1

Stencil 2

Stencil 1

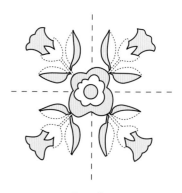

Stencil 2

Align edge of paper here.

Connect to right half.

Align edge of paper here.

Connect to left half.

Tulip and Posy Four Patch
Side Border Stencils 1–3
Enlarge pattern 200 percent.

Stencil 1
Stencil 2
Stencil 3

Stencil 1

Stencil 2

Stencil 3

Connect to right half.

Align edge of paper here.

Tulip and Posy Four Patch
Top and Bottom
Border Stencils 1–3
Enlarge pattern 200 percent.

☐ Stencil 1

☐ Stencil 2

☐ Stencil 3

Align edge of paper here.

Connect to left half.

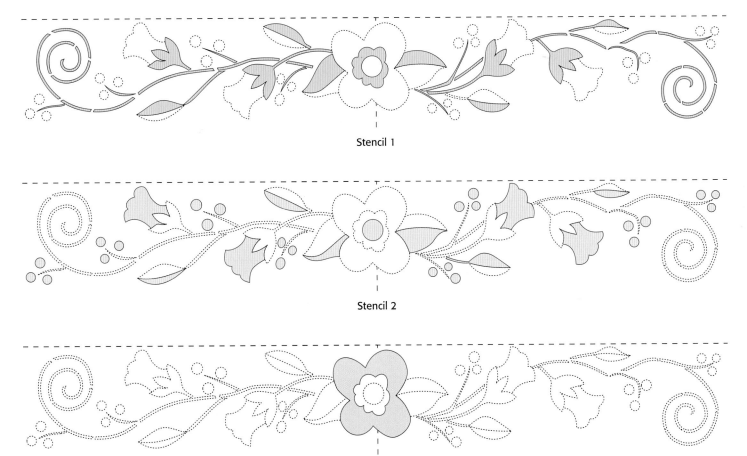

Stencil 1

Stencil 2

Stencil 3

 # Contributors

Museum of American Folk Art
2 Lincoln Square
New York, NY 10023
Phone: 212-977-7170
Fax: 212-997-8134

Old Sturbridge Village
1 Old Sturbridge Village Road
Sturbridge, MA 01566
Phone: 508-347-3362

Winterthur Museum
Route 52
Winterthur, DE 19735
Phone: 302-888-4840
Fax: 302-888 4953

# *Bibliography*

Basset, Lynne Z., and Jack Larkin. *Northern Comfort.* Nashville, Tenn.: Rutledge Press, 1998.

Kiracofe, Roderick. *The American Quilt.* New York: Clarkson Potter Publisher, 1993. Great treasury of information on history of quilts and quilting.

Nelson, Cyril I., and Carter Houck. *Treasury of American Quilts.* New York: Greenwich House. Distributed by Crown Publishers, 1984.

Orlofsky, Patsy and Myron. *Quilts in America.* New York: McGraw Hill Book Company and Abbeville Press, 1972. Absolutely the best book on quiltmaking and quilt history.

Peck, Amelia. *American Quilts and Coverlets.* New York: The Metropolitan Museum of Art and Dutton Studio Books, 1990.

Waring, Janet. *Early American Stencils.* New York: Dover Publications, 1937. All about stenciling in America.

Warren, Elizabeth V., and Sharon L. Eisenstat. *Glorious American Quilts.* New York: Penguin Studio, 1996.

About the Author

Vicki Garnas grew up in Bakersfield, California, when it was still a rural oil and farming community. After earning a degree in English from California State University at Northridge, Vicki went to work for the Los Angeles Police Department.

Vicki learned how to sew from her mother as a child and taught herself how to quilt from books. She learned to stencil after Marti Sandel shared her methods at a quilt guild meeting. Vicki has no formal art training and has developed simple ways to use freezer paper, paints, and pins to make unusual quilts.

Vicki teaches and lectures throughout the United States. She has demonstrated her techniques and shown her quilts on the *Carol Duvall Show*, the *Christopher Lowell Show*, and *Simply Quilts*. Her quilts have won numerous prizes. She is the author of *Fast-and-Fun Stenciled Quilts*, and her designs and an article on antique stenciled quilts have appeared in *American Patchwork and Quilting* magazine. She lives with her husband, Gil, and their two sons in the San Fernando Valley in Granada Hills, California.